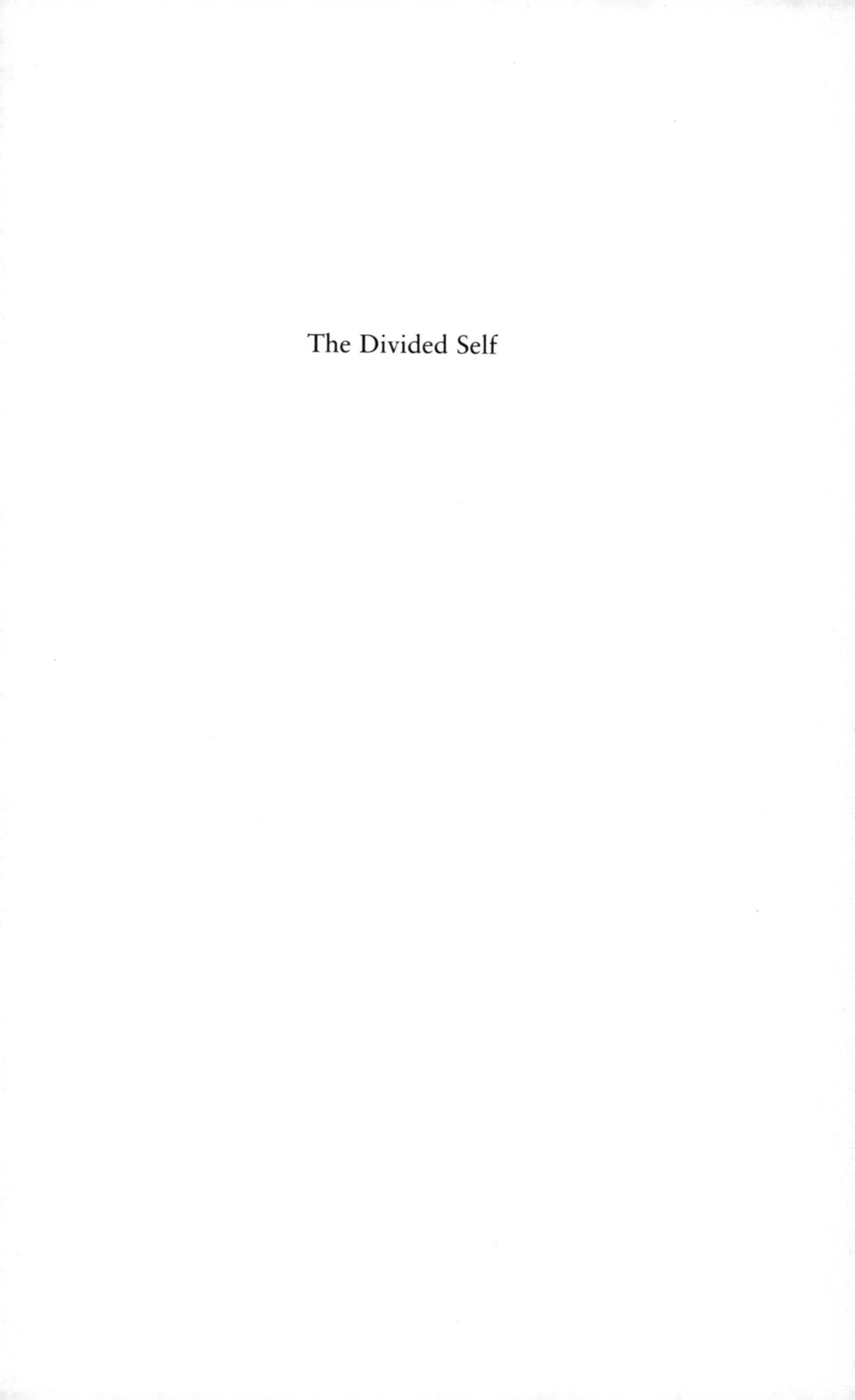

The Divided Self

THE DIVIDED SELF

Israel and the Jewish Psyche Today

David J. Goldberg

I.B. TAURIS
LONDON · NEW YORK

Published in 2006 by I.B.Tauris & Co. Ltd
6 Salem Road, London W2 4BU
175 Fifth Avenue, New York NY 10010
Website: http://www.ibtauris.com

In the United States and Canada distributed by Palgrave Macmillan,
a division of St. Martin's Press, 175 Fifth Avenue, New York NY 10010

ISBN 1 84511 054 4
EAN 978 1 84511 054 3

A full CIP record for this book is available from the British Library
A full CIP record for this book is available from the Library of Congress
Library of Congress catalog card: available

Typeset in Sabon by Dexter Haven Associates Ltd, London
Printed and bound in Great Britain by TJ International Ltd, Padstow, Cornwall

CONTENTS

INTRODUCTION

The impetus for writing this book was prompted by two widely held, rarely challenged assumptions about modern Jewish life. First, the Diaspora is in a state of terminal decline and the future of Jewry lies only in Israel. Second, there has been a disturbing rise in anti-Semitism disguised as anti-Zionism, inevitably among Arabs, but particularly in Europe among Israel's *bien pensant* critics of the new Left. Both those assumptions, it seemed to me, have been swallowed wholesale without proper analysis. It is no surprise that originally they emerged from Jerusalem, because, obviously one of Zionism's main aims is to encourage as many Jews as possible to go and live in Israel, and a handy way of deflecting criticism from Israel's continued and repressive occupation of territories captured in the 1967 war is to revive memories of the most shameful blot on the conscience of Christian Europe.

It was reasonable enough to talk about the demise of the Diaspora in the years after the Second World War, during which two-thirds of Europe's 9.2 million Jews perished as victims of the Nazi Holocaust, and the bulk of those who survived were locked behind the Soviet Union's Iron Curtain. It is no longer true today. There has been a marked renewal of European Jewish life, partly as a result of the collapse of the Soviet empire. Germany, of all countries, has the fastest-growing Jewish population in Europe, of around 150,000 people, with more than 60,000 Russian immigrants and rebuilt communities in all the major cities. In Russia itself there has been a remarkable upsurge of Jewish activity, stifled under Communism, from ultra-Orthodox synagogues to humanist groups studying Jewish culture. New congregations have been established and old ones revived in Hungary, the Czech Republic and Slovakia; even in Poland, the main Nazi killing ground of Jews, a lively community has re-emerged in Warsaw.

But received wisdom dies hard. A few years ago, a Jewish historian wrote a book entitled *Vanishing Diaspora*. After concluding his gloomy survey with the prophecy that European Jewry was doomed to a spectral existence at best, he promptly departed – not to Israel, but to a post at a university in the United States! There, 5 million Jews can enjoy a breadth, scope and variety of Jewish activity that is unsurpassed in history, at least as vigorous as anything on offer in Israel and certainly much safer physically.

The Diaspora is given short shrift in the Zionist reading of Jewish history. Its very name in Hebrew, *galut*, meaning 'exile' or 'captivity', conveys its inferior status to life in the rebuilt Jewish homeland. As I try to demonstrate, Diaspora, not statehood, has been the normative condition of Jewish history, and the adaptive lessons learnt in surviving for over two thousand years as a minority among alien cultures is at least as persuasive a guarantee of Jewish continuity as the heady delusions of power exhibited by the modern State of Israel.

Anti-Semitism, whether in its theological or economic manifestations, has been a recurring motif of the Jewish historical experience. Automatically to label criticism of Israel as anti-Semitism under another name is a crude generalisation that might be useful to Zionism's public relations industry, but it does little to help the understanding of this malign phenomenon or to stifle disquiet about the Jewish state's motives and future prospects – a disquiet shared, I might add, by increasing numbers of Israelis themselves and Diaspora Jews, to classify all of whom, in popular terminology, as 'self-hating Jews' or 'anti-Semites masquerading as anti-Zionists' would be patently absurd.

My contention is that there is a profound difference between the Israeli and the Diaspora responses to Jewish history, realpolitik and dealing with one's neighbours. It is the distinction between handling power and coping with powerlessness. We Jews have had two thousand years' experience of the latter and, since ancient times, less than sixty years' experience of the former. This has resulted in an experiential divide and a gulf of comprehension in how to relate to the outside world between Israeli Jews and the Jewish majority that has chosen to remain in the Diaspora.

In good Jewish fashion, let me illustrate the point with a story. In 1958, as a lean, fit and sun-tanned 18-year-old, I was travelling home from Israel on a ship to Marseilles after an exciting twelve months spent on a desert kibbutz riding Arab ponies and raising horses. It was a five-day voyage to Europe on a boat that seemed to be filled with giggling, blonde American girls. The situation was promising and I was making good progress with one particularly fetching example of Jewish princess pulchritude. But then, to spoil my chances, a group of recently demobbed Israeli soldiers showed up. They had been in the elite Paratroop Brigade and had fought in the 1956 Sinai campaign, with photos of dead Egyptian soldiers to show to the awe-struck American girls. I stood no chance beside these husky heroes and the biggest and brashest of them made off with the girl I had fancied. I spent the rest of the voyage either sulking or envying his lifeguard's physique, his supreme self-confidence and his simple certainty that he and his kind represented the Jewish future.

Even allowing for my petty jealousy, I was conscious of the difference between my mainly bookish, European-Jewish understanding of the world and his somewhat older, certainly more violent, yet curiously limited and parochial Israeli experience of life and people.

It crystallised when we docked at Naples for a few hours and went ashore. On his first trip abroad, my rival wanted to buy himself a good watch, then a rarity in Israel. 'Don't buy one from hawkers,' I warned him. 'They'll all be fakes and only work until you're back on board.'

'Don't worry,' he replied. 'I know how to look after myself.'

Later, back on the ship, he was proudly showing off his watch, an Omega or some such, which he had beaten down from its asking price, given his experience of bartering with Arabs. No doubt, and justifiably, he took my refusal to join in the general admiration as the reaction of a bad loser.

A few hours later, I discreetly withdrew when I came across him at the ship's rail, shaking his watch and muttering furiously at it. Then he hurled it far out to sea, sending it on its way with a common Arab curse that involved doing unspeakable things to your mother. Fortunately, he didn't see me and my grin, because otherwise I might have joined his misguided purchase. Had the phrase existed at the time, I might have murmured, 'Israelis are from Mars, Diaspora Jews are from Venus.'

How that difference between Israelis and Diaspora Jews came about, and what it signifies for Jewry today, are the themes of this book.

David J. Goldberg
London, April 2005

1 THE ZIONIST VERSION OF JEWISH HISTORY

Writing in the January 1912 issue of *Ha-Shiloah*, the journal edited by the great ideologue of Cultural Zionism, Achad Ha-Am, Joseph Luidor (who would be murdered by Arabs in Jaffa during the riots of 1921) made an explicit and provocative distinction between 'the new Jew', pioneering in the ancient homeland of Palestine, and the Diaspora Jew, who stayed behind in the countries of dispersion.

What was so novel about this distinction is that for almost nineteen hundred years, and arguably even longer, stretching back to the destruction of the First Temple and the Babylonian exile in 586 BCE, the Jews had been, and still are to this day, primarily a Diaspora people. The prophet Isaiah predicted that a 'remnant' would return from Babylonian exile and set the figure at one-tenth. It is worth noting, incidentally, that nine-tenths of the early Jewish settlers in Palestine between 1904 and 1914 either returned whence they came or wandered on to America.

We do not know what happened to the nine-tenths of Babylonian captives who elected not to follow Ezra and Nehemiah back to Jerusalem; presumably they adapted in their new land and, as Jeremiah advised them, built houses, raised families and prayed for the welfare of their rulers. In the ancient Near East, where domicile was dictated by the proximity of clan, tribe and co-religionists rather than the notion of national boundaries, people moved around fluidly and settled in whichever territory was hospitable, or at least not implacably hostile.

That was certainly the case with the Jewish fugitives from the Roman destruction of the Second Temple in 70 CE and the last, unavailing Bar Kochba rebellion against Roman rule a little more than sixty years later. They spread out around the Mediterranean. They augmented the population of Alexandria, which for two centuries had been a major Jewish metropolis, with the largest synagogue in the ancient world and long since with its own translation of the Bible, the Septuagint, for those Jews more familiar with Greek than Hebrew. Even more gravitated to Babylonia, site of their first exile, where a succession of tolerant Persian and Parthian dynasties granted large measures of autonomy to their ethnic and religious minorities. Strategic considerations may have prompted, in part, this benevolence towards the large Jewish community in Mesopotamia; the Parthian kings may have wished to counter Roman control over the Jews west of their empire. But, whatever the reason, by the second century CE the exilarch, who fancifully claimed descent from the Judean kings taken into exile by Nebuchadnezzar, was officially recognised as leader of the Jewish community and given wide-ranging powers to collect taxes, appoint Jewish judges and represent his people at court.

Despite such a favourable milieu, a clarification was needed between the dictates of Jewish law and the requirements of the ruling government. It was a leading teacher of the Babylonian Diaspora, Samuel (c. 170–250 CE), who formulated the dictum 'dina de-malchuta dina' (the law of the state is the law), whereby, in return for ceding civil authority to the government, the Jews retained control over almost all of their religious law. This formula has governed Jewish life in the Diaspora until the present.

The minority of Jews who remained in Palestine, by contrast, were eking out a forlorn existence in a cultural backwater. True, the compendium of Jewish law called the *Mishnah* was completed there around 200 CE under the editorship of a scholar known as Judah the Prince because of his wealth and easy familiarity with ruling Roman circles. But he was an exception. Significantly, Judah's most brilliant pupil, Abba, later known simply as *Rav*, meaning *the* rabbi, chose to return to Babylon. There is a Jerusalem Talmud, but it is shorter, less authoritative and less widely studied than its Babylonian equivalent. The sages of the Diaspora still deferred to their counterparts in the Holy Land, out of respect, but far outranked them – as both parties knew – in scholarship, prestige, influence and followers. After Christianity became the official religion of the Roman Empire, Jewish life in its homeland declined still further, and by the fifth century CE the Jews were almost entirely a Diaspora people.

For at least two thousand years, then, the normative condition of Jewish existence, either in the West or the East, has been that of adjusting to minority status within sometimes indifferent, often resentful, occasionally welcoming, host communities. During the course of that long experience – whether under the Roman Empire, successive popes and Holy

Roman emperors or in Muslim and Christian Spain, in the Rhineland, Poland, Constantinople or Baghdad – the Diaspora Jew learnt lessons and developed survival techniques that became characteristic: awareness, for example, that no sojourn, however initially promising, was likely to be permanent; reliance less on the current ruler, who was subject to his own variable *raisons d'état* or summary deposition, than on a network of contacts with fellow Jews, often in port cities, who could provide help when needed; a keen eye for detecting political changes, shifting alliances and business opportunities; resilience and adaptability; flexibility, based on the rabbinic admonition that it is preferable to be pliant like the willow than unbending like the palm tree; and, finally, a sense of religious identity which drew sustenance from a glorious past, put present travails into perspective and held out the hope of a redeemed future.

That was, in essence, the insecure, hand-to-mouth but remarkably prolonged existence of a subservient, homeless people who metaphorically always had their suitcases packed and were ready for flight. To which pejorative assessment the typical Diaspora Jew might have responded, with a deprecating shrug of his shoulders, by quoting the rabbinic moral to the fable about revered King David, who died in his garden on the Sabbath and could not be moved until after nightfall; that it is better to be a live dog than a dead lion.

That is why Zionism was initially so unsuccessful among the very people it sought to win over. The Jewish national movement first came to notice, albeit marginally, in the latter quarter of the nineteenth century. But it was a national movement like no other. The Greeks had fought for their independence from the Ottoman Turks. The Hungarians had sought freedom from their Austrian overlords. Garibaldi wanted a unified Italy. In each case, a people rooted in its land and sharing language, customs and folk memory in common tried to throw off a foreign yoke.

At a time when the benefits of emancipation were filtering through at last to the Jews of Europe, and even the vast Jewish population of the Russian Empire – around five million people – was seeing signs of amelioration under the relatively benign Tsar Alexander II, the early Zionists proposed a bizarre notion; that a people without its own country for two millennia should uproot, abandon hard-won civic liberties and leave to recolonise the Promised Land of the Bible.

Unsurprisingly, Zionism was a minority taste. Furthermore, its original appeal was made to the wealthy, acculturated Jews of northern Europe, asking for their help in resettling the Russian masses – the vast majority of whom showed no enthusiasm for the venture – in a strip of land negligently administered from Damascus as an outpost of the Ottoman Empire.

It was unlikely that individuals of the eminence of the Rothschilds, Montefiores or Baron de Hirsch – who manifestly had 'made it' in the wider world – would be sympathetic to Zionism's stock argument; that achieving acceptance and equal status was a foolish Jewish chimera, because European society was irredeemably tainted with the bacillus of anti-Semitism. The only solution to the 'Jewish problem' was a homeland of one's own.

When Leo Pinsker, a doctor from Odessa and first president of the *Chibbat Zion* (Love of Zion) movement, whose assimilatory hopes for Russian Jewry had been dashed by the pogroms of 1881, went to see Adolf Jellinek, Vienna's foremost rabbi, and described his mental turmoil over recent events, the rabbi put a consoling arm around his shoulder and told him to take a rest cure in Italy, where the Arch of Titus and other ancient ruins would comfort him with the knowledge that thus perished all of Israel's persecutors. 'This too will pass' was the stoic, religiously imbued attitude with which Jews traditionally responded to adversity. It had all happened before to God's Chosen People. The 1492 expulsion from Spain was but a replay of the Exodus from Judea (the Roman name for the region) after 70 CE. The mid-seventeenth-century massacres of Ukrainian Jewry by the Cossack Bogdan Chmielnitski were a rerun of the Crusades, which in turn echoed the slaughter of the pious by Antiochus Epiphanes before the Maccabees won their glorious victory in 165 BCE.

Usually living on the margins of society throughout the Middle Ages and beyond, the Jew had a curiously a-historical view of past and present. From the destruction of the Second Temple until the French Revolution, it was Rabbinic Judaism that effectively guided, controlled and arbitrated Jewish communal life. For the rabbis, who viewed history through the ineluctable prism of three key archetypes (God, Torah and Israel), every event was evaluated according to how it measured up to those theological motifs. That God had chosen Israel was a given. Why, then, had the Jews suffered so grievously? Obviously, on account of their sins, of failing to observe properly the injunctions of God's greatest gift to them, the Torah. Therefore they had been banished from their land, with all consequent tribulations, and fulfilment of the Messianic promise of return would come about only when Israel mended her ways. By contrast, Zionism was an impious, secular strategy, trying to force the Almighty's hand. In the meantime, 'Sufferance', as Shylock put it, 'is the badge of our tribe'.

But sufferance is not a synonym for passivity, as Shylock himself well demonstrated. The conventional rabbinic view was to regard Jewish history as one long weeping by the waters of Babylon, and the Zionists appropriated this convenient motif to validate their own enterprise. It has become the standard version of Jewish history, as disseminated by Zionist educational agencies in Israel and taught in religion schools and youth movements throughout the Diaspora.

As long ago as 1928, Salo Baron, the leading Jewish historian of the twentieth century, criticised this 'lachrymose' evaluation of the Diaspora experience as an unremitting saga of pain and persecution.[1] In recent years, much scholarly work has been done to redress the balance and paint a fairer picture of the totality of Diaspora history, which has had and continues to have many sunny interludes to offset the long periods of suffering. Although powerless in the sense of lacking the usual mechanisms whereby minorities could hope to sway government policy, Diaspora Jewry was often astute enough to safeguard itself by less obvious means. At times, influence, whether economic, commercial or strategic, can be more subtly effective than overt power.

The Zionist counter to this argument is that all such sunny interludes were transient and that the futile expectation of constructing a normal Jewish life in the Diaspora, even in the most favourably receptive of societies, was dealt its death blow by the Nazi Holocaust. Had there been a Jewish state in the 1930s, the Holocaust would not have been allowed to happen, and the existence of the State of Israel now ensures that such a catastrophe will never happen again. The most recent proponent of this argument was Ariel Sharon, Israel's prime minister, when he told an audience of international statesmen in March 2005 at the opening of a new museum at Yad Vashem, the Holocaust memorial in Jerusalem: 'The State of Israel is the only place in the world where Jews have the right and the strength to defend themselves by themselves. It is the only guarantee that the Jewish people will never again know a Holocaust.'

For many years after the Second World War, this assumption was accepted unquestioningly. Zionism had become the new, consolatory religion of almost all Jews. The word went forth from Jerusalem, and few – least of all the *agadim* (a derogatory term in Israel for Holocaust survivors, from the Hebrew acronym 'people of the mournful Diaspora') – presumed to take issue with the received wisdom when it was delivered by rabbis in their pulpits, educators, press officers and non-Jewish candidates seeking votes in an election. The survival of the Jewish people after the Holocaust became inextricably bound up with the survival of the State of Israel, and Emil Fackenheim, an eminent Jewish theologian, formulated a popular 614th. Commandment to add to the 613 traditionally counted in the Torah – that Hitler must not be granted a posthumous victory.[2]

But now, sixty years on from the Holocaust, and with no disrespect to its six million Jewish victims, whose memory has been appropriated for a variety of questionable causes, it should be possible to consider rationally whether or not the Zionist contention is valid.

The first thing to say is that we Jews have got ourselves caught on the horns of a dilemma. If, as we generally claim, the Holocaust was unique in its intention, scope and scientific implementation, then the slogan 'Never Again' is a tautology; by definition, a unique event cannot happen again. If, on the other hand, the Holocaust was simply the largest and most horrific example of the all-too-frequent human propensity for genocide and ethnic cleansing, then the pious hope expressed on the walls of every Holocaust museum and exhibition that we should learn from the past in order not to repeat it is similarly meaningless. Good intentions sound futilely Panglossian when confronted with hard evidence to the contrary.

Perhaps we can also dispose of the proposition that the existence of a tiny Jewish state in the 1930s would have averted the worst of the Holocaust. How? By bringing diplomatic pressure to bear on Hitler? The world's largest, most active Jewish community in the world's most powerful country, America, was spectacularly unsuccessful in achieving that. By landing troops in Russia and Poland during the killing years in order to halt the *Wehrmacht*'s advance? The idea is ludicrous.

The best a Jewish state could have aspired to was to offer a haven for fleeing refugees. How would neighbouring Arab countries, implacably opposed to the Jewish entity in their midst, have responded to that? We know how violently they reacted to any increase in Jewish immigration during the years of the British Mandate.

The speculations are endless, but one fact is clear. Powerlessness took a terrible toll on the Jewries of Europe under Nazi domination; but power, too, in the form of modern Jewish statehood, has demonstrated its limitations. The Jews have had over two thousand years' experience of coping with powerlessness and less than sixty years' experience of handling power. There are profound cultural and experiential differences between the respective responses of Diaspora Jews and Israelis to Jewish history. That is why we are in danger of becoming two peoples divided by a common language.

2 RELATIVISM AND ABSOLUTISM IN BIBLICAL TIMES

History is in the eye of the beholder. As the Italian philosopher Benedetto Croce put it, 'All history is contemporary history', which is to say, we view the past through the lens of the present and read history by the light of our own particular philosophy, ideology, life experiences and current concerns.

So it is with Jewish history. Different starting points will suggest different lessons. The devout Jew will take from Jewish history the message that God has a special and enduring relationship with His covenant people. This accounts for their miraculous survival against all odds and return to their ancient homeland. The cosmopolitan, religiously progressive Jew will emphasise instead Judaism's universal values, reinterpreting the Chosen People concept in terms of the 'Jewish Mission' and citing Isaiah's call to be 'a light unto the nations' as proof text. The religious Jewish nationalist, usually from Brooklyn or New Jersey when interviewed on TV from a West Bank settlement, will regard extending the modern State of Israel's boundaries as fulfilment of the divine promise made to Abraham, Isaac, Jacob and their descendants. The irreligious, Israeli-born, kibbutz-raised *Sabra* will derive from exile and homelessness the Zionist lesson that only by having a land of one's own can one normalise Jewish existence, because – using another biblical text, from Numbers, chapter 23, as confirmation – Israel is forever destined to be 'a people that shall dwell alone'. The secular Jew might regard Jewish history as a burden and prefer to live anonymously as a citizen of the world, hopefully without any identifying characteristics to mark him out.

For Jews of whatever background, religion and history are inextricably linked. The culturally and geographically disparate Jewries of the world share by way of common identity a *religious* heritage stretching back to the first patriarch, Abraham, and incorporating the Exodus from Egypt, the Giving of the Law on Mt Sinai, the Promised Land, prophetical teachings of brotherhood and social justice, the destruction of the two Temples, exile and the hope of eventual Messianic redemption. Deal with it how he will, no Jew can avoid the fact that being Jewish is also a religious definition as much as a cultural, ethnic or national one.

Judaism, the religion of the Jewish people, oscillates between the two poles of universalism and particularism. Abundant texts can be cited from prophetic, rabbinic, mediaeval and modern literature in support of either position. Depending on time, place and circumstances, prophets, rabbis, mediaeval philosophers and post-Enlightenment thinkers have emphasised one strand of Jewish theology or the other. All such statements have to be sifted and judged according to context. The confident, Walt Whitman-like hymns to the Republic of American Reform rabbis living in the land of promise in the latter quarter of the nineteenth century no more 'prove' that Judaism is an outward-looking religion concerned with the fate of all humanity than the bitter threnodies of Solomon Ibn Verga (a Spanish Jew exiled in 1492 and forced to live as a *converso*, who in the 1520s compiled an account of every Jewish persecution from Second Temple times to his own day in a book entitled *Shevet Yehudah*)[1] 'prove' that Judaism is a self-absorbed religion concerned only with the fate of its own. In a history as lengthy and with such an extensive literature as that of the Jews, there are plenty of examples of both tendencies.

Because no interpretation of the past can be truly objective, whatever historians may claim, it is only proper to declare any special interests. Mine are those of a liberal Jew by religious definition, with – not automatically the same thing – a strong commitment to the ideology of liberalism that has been the prevalent political discourse of Western societies since the French Revolution. The golden mean, the middle path, moderation in all things, the primacy of Reason, tolerance of diversity, freedom of speech, belief and opinion – these are the religious and philosophical precepts that most appeal to liberals, plus, for Jewish liberals, a keen attachment to the benefits that resulted from the Enlightenment, enabling us to escape from the ghetto and take our place as equal citizens of democratic societies. That is why posing hypothetical questions about whether the Enlightenment was a good or bad thing for the Jews, as religious traditionalists, fearful of the decline in belief, are wont to do, infuriates us – in so far as liberals permit themselves to be infuriated...

This liberal outlook provides yet another perspective from which to consider Jewish history. It can be analysed not so much as a struggle for supremacy between the contrasting theological categories of universalism and particularism but as an ongoing debate between two differing political formulas for Jewish survival; on the one hand, what we will call the *relativist* approach, and, on the other, the *absolutist* approach. The relativist views strategy, foreign alliances and the use or withholding of force in terms of what is realistically obtainable, politics being the art of the possible. The absolutist makes no concession to such pragmatic calculations but stakes all on uncompromising principle.

Perhaps the best, least contentious place to begin testing this theory is in the Bible itself and the narrative it records of Jewish sovereignty from the time of the Davidic kingdom until the destruction of the First Temple in 586 BCE. It is both ancient and modern Israel's geopolitical destiny to be located in the border region between larger powers to the north and south. For most of the time from the Israelite conquest of Canaan (c. 1200 BCE) until the destruction of the Second Temple (70 CE), the Jewish inhabitants of a small land lived in the shadow of great empires, rarely enjoying national independence.

Under King David (c. 1000–960 BCE), Israel achieved a unity, military capability and territorial size the like of which would never again be equalled. Later generations came to idealise this ambitious, ruthless, sensual and also deeply spiritual man as a great folk hero from whose lineage the Messiah himself would come.

David's achievements were exceptional. An outstanding military leader but also a shrewd diplomat who bought, curried or won favour, he consolidated his hold on power after the death of King Saul by cunningly choosing the Jebusite city of Jerusalem as his capital. Situated halfway between the fractious Israelite tribes of the north and the south, yet in the territory of neither, it was an ideal location from which to rule. David turned Jerusalem into the religious as well as the political capital of his kingdom.

Securely established as ruler of the country, he embarked on a policy of military expansion that within a few years transformed Israel into the region's foremost power. Conquered peoples were incorporated into his regime, sometimes as mercenaries, and paid him tribute to subsidise further colonial ventures. Abroad, his empire extended from Phoenicia in the west to the Arabian desert in the east and from the river Orontes in the north to the Gulf of Aqaba in the south. At home, the economy flourished and people prospered; no wonder that, centuries later, people would hark back nostalgically in myth and legend to the grandeur that had been.

David's successor was neither the oldest nor the most popular but certainly the most astute of his sons. Solomon was not a military hero like his father, but nevertheless he managed to maintain David's empire almost intact, usually by judicious alliances, many of them sealed by marriage. Thus it was that a pharaoh's daughter of the Twenty-first Dynasty became one of his several foreign wives.

Although folk tales about Solomon's wisdom credit him with writing the biblical Book of Proverbs, answering the Queen of Sheba's riddles and being able to converse with animals, his true genius lay in his commercial abilities. He recognised the economic significance of Israel's position astride the major trade routes of Egypt and Arabia and exploited it to the full. A merchant fleet voyaged afar from its Red Sea base, bringing back gold, silver, rare woods, jewels, ivory and even, for his majesty's amusement, monkeys. Taxes and duties from the overland caravan trade flowed into the royal treasury. The largest refinery known in the ancient Orient was built at Ezion Geber, where copper was hammered into ingots for export and refined for domestic use. A further lucrative sideline was the monopoly on Cilician horses and Egyptian chariots, both the best of their kind.

This unparalleled affluence was reflected in ambitious building projects, culminating in the Jerusalem Temple for the God of Israel, one of the wonders of the ancient world. In an atmosphere of material plenty and military security, the arts and sciences flourished; a sophisticated poetic and prose literature developed that would become the basis of the Pentateuch, as well as the vivid narratives of court history in the books of II Samuel and I Kings.

But not even Solomon, for all his vaunted wisdom, could maintain the good times indefinitely. His palatial court, large army, burgeoning bureaucracy and grandiose building schemes came at a heavy cost. Stratagems for raising money grew harsher and more desperate. The land was reorganised into twelve administrative districts, each one obliged to provide the royal upkeep for a month. Solomon even began selling off territory, ceding towns along the Bay of Acre to his old trading partner, the king of Tyre.

Like his father before him, Solomon ruled for approximately forty years (c. 960–920 BCE). His latter days were marked by increasing popular resentment at the burden of taxation and an open, quickly crushed rebellion. It was his son and inheritor, Rehoboam, who would pay the price.

In Jerusalem, the royal city, Rehoboam was accepted without demur as the descendant of the Davidic line, but when he journeyed to Shechem (modern Nablus), to be recognised as king of Israel by the northern tribes, the response was cooler. As the price of their allegiance, tribal representatives demanded that the burdens imposed by his father should be lightened.

Rehoboam was an arrogant and reckless young man. Instead of heeding the prudent advice of court elders to listen to the people's complaints, he chose to be guided by the *jeunesse dorée* of his entourage, the ancient counterparts of those spoilt young bloods nowadays who race around Beirut and Riyadh in their customised sports cars. When the representatives returned for his answer, Rehoboam promised them that, whereas his father had taxed them hard, he would tax them harder; where Solomon had chastised them with whips, he would chastise them with scorpions.

Angrily, the tribal representatives announced their secession, forced the king to flee and proclaimed in his stead a man called Jeroboam who had recently returned from Egyptian exile, whither he had fled after the failed rebellion against Solomon.

So it was that the unified kingdom and far-flung empire determinedly built up by David and shrewdly maintained by Solomon came to an end. Its glory had been brief, about seventy years. The historical pattern was set. From now on, in north and south, two separate yet entwined states – sometimes in uneasy alliance, sometimes actively hostile to each other – would face a long, bruising struggle to maintain a tenuous independence from rapacious neighbours, until the northern kingdom of Israel was destroyed by the Assyrians in 722 BCE, and almost 150 years later the southern kingdom of Judah fell to Babylonian assault.

Our main historical sources for this period are the unknown writers of the books of Kings and Chronicles and the prophets who had books named after them, such as Amos, Hosea, Isaiah, Micah and Jeremiah. The thing to bear in mind about these named and unnamed sources is that *they were all absolutists*. That is to say, they had one simple, unwavering test whereby the kingdoms of Israel and Judah, and their policies, were judged. Had they done good or had they done evil in the sight of the Almighty? Had the people stayed faithful to the Covenant? There could be no compromise about meeting God's demands. After all, first and foremost the Bible is a justification of God's relationship with Israel and why, if required, He was compelled to punish His sinful people.

That is what makes so fascinating, and sometimes surprising at first sight, the judgement passed by biblical authors on the succession of kings and usurpers who tried to guide their countries through these turbulent times. The ones who managed to maintain their kingdom intact are sometimes reviled, while those who chose to go down fighting rather than compromise are not necessarily praised. The biblical authors and prophets may have been absolutists in their zealous obedience to what they perceived as the will of God and impossibly exacting in the standards they set for monarchs and their subjects; but they varied widely in their assessments of whether a particular ruler acted prudently or not in safeguarding the religious health and physical security of God's Chosen People. In that respect, and not looking back with the benefit of hindsight but reacting to current national exigencies, prophets such as Amos, Micah, the first Isaiah and Jeremiah demonstrated a wide range of political responses, from unwavering absolutism to a relativist 'feel' for switching allegiances when tactically beneficial. We shall look in the next chapter at some examples of this process at work, with particular reference to the ministries of Isaiah and Jeremiah.

3 DEPENDENCY ON MORE POWERFUL NEIGHBOURS

Until the destruction of the Temple by Nebuchadnezzar in 586 BCE, the history of the northern kingdom of Israel (also called Samaria in the Bible or occasionally Ephraim) and the southern kingdom of Judah, as told in I and II Kings and II Chronicles, is a complicated, navel-gazing narrative from which the naïve reader might gain the impression that this small strip of divided territory was at the epicentre of the ancient world; as indeed it was for the biblical authors, given their commitment to evaluating every event by the light of God's relationship with His people, Israel.

But, in the context of wider history, one distinctive motif becomes apparent – that *empire* was the enduring political reality of the ancient Middle East, and small nations such as Israel and Judah could only achieve or maintain a precarious independence during periods of imperial decline. Their usual recourse was to strike alliances with the dominant empire as a vassal state. The upside for a strategically situated country such as Israel was that she could seek advantages by playing off one imperial power against another; the downside was that she came under increased suspicion as a result and any glimmerings of revolt would be suppressed ruthlessly.

It mattered little to the overall picture that, after the initial contrast between vigorous, popular Jeroboam and sulky, deposed Rehoboam, Israel in the north suffered by and large from a series of incompetent and corrupt leaders, whereas Judah in the south generally benefited from an able Davidic succession; or that smaller Judah was located around Jerusalem, a natural defensive stronghold, where the Temple evoked loyalty and religious fervour from all, while larger Samaria was easier to invade and vulnerable to outside religious influences, especially fertility cults, idolatry and Baal worship. In the long run, neither country could hope to withstand the empires of Egypt, Assyria or Babylonia.

That is illustrated by events leading up the fall of Israel in 722 BCE. Superficially, the northern kingdom had attained new heights of prosperity under the long rule of Jeroboam II (786–746), but anarchy ensued after his death. Five kings followed in quick succession between 746 and 736, three of them seizing power by violence and none with a legitimate claim to the throne. The prophet Hosea paints a vivid picture of those chaotic years, law and order having broken down, the highways dangerous to travel, neither life nor property safe.

While Israel was collapsing from within and Hosea was proclaiming her impending doom, Assyria's new king, Tiglath-Pileser III, was laying the foundations of a great empire. He pushed westwards beyond the Euphrates. The ruler of Israel, a former army officer called Pekah ben Ramaliah, who had come to power after a Macbeth-like regicide, foolishly joined with Damascus and a number of Philistine cities in an anti-

Assyrian coalition. Judah's king, Ahaz, kept aloof, but the coalition partners could not tolerate a neutral neighbour and invaded Judah from the north, while an Edomite insurrection in the south drove the Judeans from Eilat.

In desperation, Ahaz called on Assyria for help, offering up lavish booty. The prophet Isaiah warned him against such a move, urging calmness and correctly forecasting that within a few years the northern kingdom would be destroyed. As a sign of God's protection Isaiah made his notorious promise, so avidly fastened on by fundamentalist Christian readers of the Bible as a reference to Jesus, that a young woman (not a virgin, as both the Septuagint and Vulgate translations of the Hebrew word have been incorrectly understood) would give birth to a child called Immanuel. Ahaz would not listen to him and Isaiah, in a huff, retired from public ministry for several years. His absolutist credo had been rejected.

Tiglath-Pileser was more than happy to help Ahaz out. His army routed the coalition forces, captured great swathes of territory and carried off captives. Pekah, whose folly had brought on the disaster, was murdered. The new ruler, Hoshea ben Elah (732–724), won temporary respite by surrendering and paying swingeing tribute.

When Tiglath-Pileser died in 727, the truncated kingdom of Israel made one last attempt to throw off Assyrian domination. Hoshea allied with an Egyptian princeling and withheld his annual contribution. Assyria's new leader, Shalmaneser V, reacted promptly. He invaded, occupied the land and took Hoshea prisoner. The city of Samaria held out under siege for three years, during which time Shalmaneser died. His successor, Sargon II, captured the city in 722 and deported its inhabitants to upper Mesopotamia and Medea. In time they merged with the local population and forgot their national identity, which had never been strong and always prone to religious dilution, becoming the 'ten lost tribes'. Thus did the northern kingdom of Israel disappear from the pages of history.

Ahaz held on in the south, but the price of survival, as he allowed pagan cults and superstitions to flourish unchecked and built an altar to Assyrian gods in the Temple itself, was not worth paying, in the estimation of Isaiah. He was more favourably disposed towards Ahaz's son and successor, Hezekiah, who closed down the pagan shrines and undertook a cultic purge. Hezekiah was more willing to listen to Isaiah's advice.

A failed rebellion against Sennacherib in 701 proved costly, forcing Hezekiah to strip the Temple and the royal treasury for tribute, as well as sending his daughters to Nineveh as concubines. Ten years later, Hezekiah tried again, in alliance with Babylon and Egypt. As confidently as before, Sennacherib moved against the rebels, subduing Babylon with great ferocity then marching on Jerusalem. The aged prophet repeated his mantra that God would not forsake Zion, and, this time, the king stayed resolute. A mysterious epidemic, perhaps bubonic plague, devastated Sennacherib's army, which 'melted like snow in the glance of the Lord!' The Judeans celebrated their remarkable deliverance.

The fate of Israel, and the contrasting posthumous reputations of Ahaz and Hezekiah, might lead one to suppose that, for the biblical authors, the only test was whether or not a ruler was willing to put his trust in divine protection. If yes, his kingdom would survive. If no, Assyria, Babylon and Egypt, the three competing empires, would themselves be used as unwitting instruments of God's vengeance to punish the wicked kingdom. But of course it was not that simple. For example, Hezekiah's son and successor, Manasseh, reigned for forty-five years. A shrewd accomodationist, he retained the trust of successive Assyrian rulers after Sennacherib and managed to keep his kingdom intact – cause for approval, one might think. But in the biting verdict of the author of II Kings, chapter 21, he was the worst king ever to sit on David's throne. His sin was to set up altars to the Assyrian deities, permitting sacred prostitution and fertility rites within the Temple itself; but for all that, by such flattering obeisance towards their overlords, he and his subjects survived to disprove the notion that God safeguarded only the righteous among His people.

If we fast-forward one hundred years, a totally different perspective applies when Jeremiah is the prophet and Jerusalem is once again looking hopefully to Egypt as an ally against Babylon. Jeremiah explicitly repudiated Isaiah's article of faith that God would never abandon Zion. It had become a dogma of inviolability that filled the Judeans with false optimism and underlay the disastrous foreign policy choices of King Jehoiakim and his successor, Zedekiah. So contentious was Jeremiah's preaching that he was beaten, imprisoned and threatened with death. By any conventional judgement, Jeremiah was a traitor who gave comfort to the enemy, never more so than when the inhabitants of Jerusalem were holding out with doomed bravery against the besieging Babylonians and the prophet was walking the city walls telling them that their defence was hopeless. In reality, he was a perspicacious observer with a conviction no less strong than Isaiah's (Jeremiah purchased a plot of land outside Jerusalem, as a sign of his faith that God would restore the captives) but with a more flexible and less obdurate approach to politics.

A weak, vacillating man, King Zedekiah was torn between contrary advice; that of Jeremiah, who counselled submission to overwhelming Babylonian power in order to retrieve something from the catastrophe; and that of other priests, prophets and courtiers, who based their resistance on faith in divine intervention. This time it was the relativist Jeremiah whose advice was rejected and the absolutists, unwilling to learn from experience, who led Judah into three major deportations of its citizens between 597 and 581 BCE and the traumatic destruction of the First Temple in 586. Zedekiah himself was blinded and taken in chains to Babylonia, having been forced to witness the execution of his sons.

The fate of Jeremiah is unknown. The most popular theory is that he accompanied those fugitives who fled to Egypt. What is certain is that, in chapter 29 of the biblical book bearing his name, he sent a letter to the captives in Babylon, encouraging them to rebuild their lives there and pray for the welfare of their adopted country. It was advice consistent with his general approach, always to adapt to circumstances rather than trying to alter the Almighty's inexorable will.

The residue in Jerusalem was not so phlegmatic. Because they regarded him as a quisling, diehards assassinated Nebuchadnezzar's appointed governor, Gedaliah, who had tried to restore a semblance of administration and normalcy to the land. In reprisal, the Babylonians deported still more of the population. The Kingdom of Judah effectively ceased to exist, sharing the exiled fate of its northern neighbour, Israel, a century and a half previously.

In determining foreign policy for both Israel and Judah, the absolutist creed had prevailed, but at a terrible cost. According to Plutarch, Pyrrhus reflected after defeating the Romans at Asculum that another such 'victory' and everything would be lost. Unfortunately, when next given the opportunity, centuries later, to take control of their destiny, the Jews demonstrated the truth of the old adage about history repeating itself.

4 LEARNING THE LESSONS OF EXILE

The price of refusing to bend the knee, as Jeremiah had advised, was deportation to Babylon of the nobles, ecclesiastics and administrative class, leaving behind a destroyed central shrine and a shattered social order. The fields lay fallow and harvests rotted as the peasant labourers fled. The Babylonians did not plant new settlers, as the Assyrians had done in Samaria. Thus Judah's estimated population of around a quarter of a million in the eighth century dwindled to about 20,000 in the aftermath of exile.

Psalm 137, one of the best known in the Bible for its opening words, 'By the waters of Babylon, there we sat down and wept', suggests the melancholy of exile, given equally famous musical form in Verdi's lilting chorus of the Hebrew slaves from *Nabucco*. In fact, though, from our meagre sources about the lives of the captives it would appear that the exiles received a sympathetic welcome in Babylon. They were neither enslaved nor treated with physical cruelty. Placed in their own settlements, they resumed their regular occupations as farmers, craftsmen and traders with obligations of service and taxation to the state. We know from chapter 25 of II Kings that in 561 BCE the former Judean king, Jehoiachin, was released from prison and granted a pension. This is corroborated by Babylonian records. It was during this time that Babylonian names, the Babylonian calendar and the Aramaic language were adopted by the Judeans. Even more importantly, although not relevant to the theme of this book, it was during the half-century of Babylonian exile that the Jewish religion, Judaism, took on the shape that it would develop in the centuries to come and the narrative and legal records of Israel's past were assembled into something like the form they would finally assume in the Bible.

Cultural assimilation while retaining religious individuality was the template for Babylonian and all subsequent Jewish exiles. The assumption in the ancient world was that subject peoples would automatically take on the *mores* of their conquerors. There was ethnic diversity, certainly, but not the multicultural options on offer in modern Western society. The *modus operandi* of imperialism was set long before the Romans perfected it – subjugate then incorporate by permitting a measure of autonomy in return for fealty.

So it was that the exiles transferred their loyalty to Cyrus, king of Persia, after his armies had conquered Babylon. In the manner of enlightened despots, he issued a decree in 538 BCE that permitted the Judeans to return to Jerusalem and rebuild their Temple. It suited his strategic goals to have an enclave of grateful Jews conveniently situated near to the Egyptian frontier.

We do not know how many or how few took up Cyrus's offer. One-tenth, Second Isaiah's estimate of the remnant who would return, sounds about right. The majority stayed put in

Babylon. By now, the generation who remembered Zion was elderly. For their children, it meant a difficult, lengthy journey with an uncertain outcome; fearful comparisons with the original Exodus from Egypt must have been irresistible. Renouncing Diaspora security in Babylon for the hazards of pioneering presaged the choice that nearly two and a half millennia later would face the first generation of Zionists.

Work on restoring the Temple began almost immediately. It was finally completed around 515 BCE, in the sixth year of Darius's reign. The decades since Cyrus's decree had been scarred by tension between returning exiles and their native kinsmen who regarded themselves as the 'true' Israel, by simmering violence with their Samaritan neighbours to the north, by unfulfilled promises of aid from the Persian court and by constant friction with colonial officials in Samaria. A Jewish nucleus eking out a precarious existence in the few square miles around its rebuilt Temple was a mere sub-district of the Persian Empire, an anonymous extra on the stage of Middle Eastern politics, where the onward march of Darius was finally halted at Marathon by the Athenians, where his successors, Xerxes and Artaxerxes, continued the fight against the Greek city states and where giant figures such as Pericles, Socrates, Plato, Sophocles, Aeschylus and ultimately, greatest and most glamorous of them all, Alexander of Macedon were making their contributions to Western civilisation.

And yet, and this is the significant point, because the Jewish returnees and subsequent generations had absorbed the lesson of First Temple history that absolutism spelt disaster, they were able to maintain tiny Judah intact for over three centuries. The Jewish polity meekly accepted its dependency on superpower goodwill and its impotence to pursue an independent foreign policy. By accommodating to imperial reality, the

Persian and early Greek periods (c. 500–200 BCE) were ones of relative calm and prosperity for Judah. In addition, internal stability enabled the Jews to embark on their own astonishing burst of religious and literary creativity. It was during these centuries that the law (Torah) given to Moses, and through him to Israel, was canonised, thereby enabling Jews, wherever they lived, to follow unwavering norms which united them in a common, supraterritorial religion. In addition, the prophetic books of Joel, Zechariah and Malachi were composed, as well as the historical narratives of I and II Chronicles, the book of Psalms, the Wisdom literature of Proverbs, the love poetry of the Song of Songs and the profound questioning of theodicy in the book of Job.

The Persian Empire was swept away, and Jews adjusted to the new order of Hellenistic civilisation that followed in the wake of Alexander's conquests. They remained submissive subjects after the death of Alexander in 323 BCE, when the Ptolemies of Egypt assumed control of Palestine, following two decades of civil war between generals competing for the Alexandrian succession. Jews enjoyed the benefits of the Greek language, now the lingua franca of the Mediterranean region, Greek architecture, science, the arts and the *Gymnasion*, in which classical ideals of education and physical grace were inculcated. More than thirty Greek cities were established in Palestine, along the coast and in the area of Transjordan. The Jewish political leadership, symbolised by the figure of the High Priest, who was regarded as the people's titular representative, was still abiding by the strategy that for three centuries had successfully avoided a repetition of the calamities of the First Temple era.

The situation did not noticeably change after 198 BCE, when the Seleucid king Antiochus III defeated the Egyptian army at Baniyas, near the headwaters of the river Jordan, and annexed Palestine. The Jews, cannily forecasting the outcome, had thrown in their lot with Antiochus, taking up arms against Ptolemy's garrison in Jerusalem. Their defection to the victorious side was duly rewarded by Antiochus, who ordered the release of Jewish soldiers captured fighting for Ptolemy, waived taxes in Jerusalem for three years and reaffirmed the religious and political privileges that Jews had enjoyed under Persian and Ptolemaic rule, including the right to live 'according to the laws of their fathers'. He also promised state aid for repairs to the Temple and favourable status for priestly personnel. Seleucid rule had begun auspiciously.

But Antiochus was no more immune than his new Jewish subjects to a power still greater than his own. He made the mistake of giving shelter to the defeated Carthaginian general Hannibal. Rome neither forgave nor forgot. A crushing military victory was confirmed by a savage peace treaty that forced Antiochus to send his son (later Antiochus IV) as a hostage to Rome and imposed a huge tribute that would financially cripple the Seleucid dynasty.

Antiochus himself was killed while plundering a temple in Elam in order to pay off the Romans, and the constant need for money was the motivating factor in Antiochus IV's disastrous meddling in internal Jewish politics. He made himself available to the highest bidder in a power struggle for the office of High Priest. Coup, assassination and counter-coup against his chosen puppet followed, tempting Antiochus to loot the Temple treasures by way of reprisal.

A year later, he overreached himself. He was marching on Alexandria in search of booty when the Romans intervened and ordered him to withdraw. Antiochus asked for time to consider, but the Roman ambassador famously drew a circle round him in the sand and told him to make up his mind there and then.

Jerusalem was made to pay for the king's public humiliation. The city was looted and partially destroyed, and a Syrian garrison was installed in a citadel called the Acra. The Acra was not simply a military stronghold; it was an autonomous colony of Hellenised pagans and imitative Jews, a Greek *polis,* in the very heart of Jerusalem.

This was a jarring affront to Jewish sensibilities, but worse followed. Temple worship was suspended, to be replaced with pagan cults, and the practice of Judaism was forbidden on pain of death. The circumcision of male children was likewise proscribed. Then, in December 167 BCE, an altar to Zeus was erected in the Temple itself and swine's flesh offered on it.

At this distance of time, it is hard to understand what goaded Antiochus to impose such crudely insensitive and oppressive measures. It was quite contrary to the tested Greek method of dealing with subject peoples and respecting their religious customs. Perhaps Antiochus had lost his reason. Certainly, he was mocked by satirists as *Epimanes* (the Madman) rather than his own chosen soubriquet of *Epiphanes* (the God Manifest).

Whatever his motives, it was the Jewish response that is significant. Initial reaction was neither unanimous nor effective. Those Jews who embraced Greek culture, comprising the upper strata of society, were dumbfounded by such a radical departure from Hellenism's norms of progressive assimilation and accepted the decrees, no doubt hoping that they were a temporary aberration. The rest of the population, conservative and traditionalist, had neither the means nor the organisation to resist. Of those who objected, the small and scrupulously law-observing sect of *Chasidim* (pious ones) was massacred because of their refusal to bear arms on the Sabbath.

The dilemma of how to respond neatly encapsulated the perennial Jewish tension between accommodation and resistance, powerlessness and power. When guerrilla resistance did eventually cohere around the leadership of the Hasmonean clan, it was initially confined to the struggle for control of the High Priest's office, even if fuelled by nationalist and religious sentiment.

In popular legend, the victory of Judas, nicknamed Maccabeus (the hammer), and his brothers against the Seleucid armies is celebrated at the annual festival of Chanukkah as the deliverance of Judaism from the dark forces of Hellenism seeking to destroy it, when the few stood against the many and right triumphed over might. The reality was more complicated.

The Hasmoneans were a priestly family, and their primary concern was to wrest the high priesthood for themselves. That this was so is demonstrated by the fact that when Jonathan, the youngest brother, was recognised by a claimant to the Seleucid throne as High Priest in 154 BCE (his rival having previously offered Jonathan the bait of provincial governor) an uneasy truce followed and the overall authority of the Seleucid kingdom was reaffirmed. This status quo lasted until 142, when Jonathan was captured by guile and put to death. In retaliation, the last surviving brother, Simon, resumed the revolt and forced the evacuation of the Acra in Jerusalem, the hated symbol of Seleucid rule. Two years later, in the autumn of 140, Simon's authority was ratified by an assembly of priests, elders and the people, who confirmed him in the combined role of High Priest, military commander and ethnarch (ruler). A struggle lasting nearly thirty years had been for the strictly limited goal of establishing one priestly family as religious and civilian overlords of Judea. Thus did the Hasmonean dynasty come into being. A formal alliance with Rome and the minting of the first coins ever issued by the Jewish state were the tangible fruits of newly acquired independence.

It lasted less than eighty years. The authority of the Hasmoneans, especially the legitimacy of their claim to the high priesthood, was never fully established. The Pharisees, in particular, challenged the manner in which one family had arrogated to itself all the trappings of royalty. Simon's son and successor, John Hyrcanus, ruled for thirty-one years, until 104 BCE, but after his death internecine struggles and the simmering ideological rivalry between the two socially and religiously conflicting groups of Pharisees and Sadducees led to internal disintegration and civil war. When two brotherly claimants for the succession, Aristobolus II and Hyrcanus II, took up arms, it provided the Roman general, Pompey, with a pretext for direct intervention. In 63 BCE he occupied the Temple after a three-month siege, recognised Hyrcanus as High Priest but not as king and banished Aristobolus and his family to Rome. Judea was reduced once again to the status of a vassal, this time of Rome.

Thus did the later Hasmoneans squander their patrimony and why it is that they received distinctly cool treatment in subsequent rabbinic literature. After Julius Caesar's assassination in 44 BCE, they made a last attempt to return to power, but the Romans, who always preferred to exert control through local rulers, sent in the legions and imposed Herod, the hated son of a forced Idumean convert, as their client king and 'an ally and friend of the Roman people'.

The Hasmonean interlude provides a classic case study of the extent to which any tiny country, the colony of a powerful empire, can presume to control its own destiny as an independent entity. Two ingredients, at least, are essential in order to allow a degree of manoeuvrability; first, an internal leadership united in its goals and policy, and second, the possession of enough strategic or commercial value to the dominant power to be permitted a certain level of indulgent latitude when acting unilaterally. Neither of these factors applied during the Hasmonean period, which is why Judea came under the repressive domination of Rome and its people would look back nostalgically to benign Persian and Greek rule. Within seventy years, Rome would test to breaking point the tension between Jewish relativists and absolutists over how to respond to external power and one's own powerlessness.

5 THE ROMAN DISASTER

Herod put to death his beloved wife, Mariamne, three sons and any relative whom he suspected of plotting against him. 'It were better to be such a man's swine than his son,' was the comment of the emperor, Augustus, about Herod's jealous paranoia. His reign ended in a miasma of intrigue, assassinations and repression. When he finally passed away in 4 BCE after an agonising terminal illness, crowds came out into the streets to celebrate.

Herod is remembered in popular legend as an ogre, arguably the worst ruler ever to govern the Jews, and of foreign ancestry to boot. In fact, between terrifying bouts of pathological excess, he displayed ability and acumen, imposing a precarious stability upon Judea for his Roman overlords. He dug deeply into his own pockets to help the needy during the famine years of 24 and 23 BCE, and his ambitious building projects, including a magnificent new seaport at Caesarea and extensive improvements to the Temple and its environs, provided employment for large sections of the population. It was Herod who constructed the fortress of Masada, which stands to this day as a symbol of the divide between accommodationists and absolutists. He cannot be held solely responsible for the bitterly confrontational tendencies that gathered momentum during and after his reign, and led, in 66 CE, to open rebellion against Rome and the tragedy that reached its apogee in 73 with the alleged mass suicide, rather than capture, of 960 zealot defenders at Masada.

In addition to the existing factions of Pharisees and Sadducees, who jostled for control of the supreme legislative assembly (the Sanhedrin), and the Essenes, who had withdrawn to their desert communities to await the end of days, an unpredictable new group had emerged on the Judean scene. Loosely composed of revolutionaries, zealots and other radical, Messianic sects, this new coalition threatened imperial stability with its fervent longing for the deliverance of Israel from foreign yoke by an ideal, anointed king of Davidic descent and its urgent belief that the apocalyptic times which would usher in God's kingdom on earth were imminent. The first century CE was the frenzied heyday of Jewish eschatological yearning, as Roman rule tightened its grip and only some extraordinary deliverance seemed likely to lift it.

The Pharisees and Sadducees tended only to challenge Roman domination if their religious sensibilities were offended, and Roman rule, on the whole, was careful to respect Jewish religious feelings. But the combustible brew of a succession of inept, corrupt Roman procurators, a fragmented Jewish leadership and ideologically inflamed Jewish revolutionaries spoiling for a fight presaged only one outcome.

In 64 CE, civil disorder spread and riots flared throughout the country. Belatedly, Rome despatched the legate of Syria to reassert imperial authority. As his legion marched through the mountain pass of Beth Horon, it was cut to pieces by Jewish rebels. The die had been cast.

Nero put Vespasian in charge of pacifying Judea. By the winter of 67, all of Galilee and northern Palestine were once more under Roman control. In the spring of 68, Vespasian marched southward, systematically cutting off Jerusalem. He was poised to begin its siege when news arrived of Nero's suicide. Before hurrying home to claim the emperorship, Vespasian handed over military command to his son, Titus.

A few days before Passover in April 70 CE, the Romans set up camp outside the walls of Jerusalem. It took six months to subdue the city, as its defenders fought courageously against heavily superior numbers. On 28 August, the Temple was stormed and destroyed by flames. After another month of fighting, the whole city was in Roman hands and resistance ceased. Titus then razed Jerusalem, except for the towers of Herod's palace, and thousands of Jews were enslaved and their property confiscated.

The diehards still held out, chiefly at the Dead Sea fortress of Masada, the last stronghold to fall, in April 73. An alleged mass suicide was the final, despairing gesture of those who had risked all and lost. The hopeless struggle against Roman might had been a national conflict, sucking in every stratum of Jewish society, including the Nazarenes (early Christian Jews), Hellenised aristocrats, fanatical zealots, even the ruling family of the tiny Mesopotamian kingdom of Adiabene, who had recently converted to Judaism and come to live in Jerusalem. The climax at Masada was proof positive to some, notably the Pharisees, that absolutism in the face of imperial domination was self-defeating and negotiated compromise was the only sane course. Others, paradoxically, chose to see in Masada the glorious vindication of an all-or-nothing policy that prefers annihilation to settlement. It is a debate that still resonates in Jewish political discourse to this day. During the nuclear proliferation of the late 1980s, an Israeli government minister declared that Israel would not be the first country in the Middle East to use nuclear weapons – but she would be the last.

Reflecting on the breakdown of internal authority and the anarchy that had prevailed during the war against Rome, when the dagger had been the favoured weapon for settling scores in the teeming alleyways of Jerusalem – a later generation of rabbis declared that the Temple had been destroyed because of 'groundless hatred' among the Jews themselves. It was an attempt to find a plausible, self-censuring rationale for the destruction and exile that had resulted. But, because their predecessors had been as heavily involved – and bitterly divided – as everyone else in Jerusalem, it smacks rather of special pleading. The fact was that the extremists, rabbis among them, had prevailed, and it was their refusal to countenance any form of accommodation with Rome that led to catastrophe.

Because the destruction of the Temple in 70 CE resulted in the priesthood losing both its religious function and its political authority, the way was clear for the Pharisaic sect and their successors, the rabbis, to assume leadership of national life. History was glossed to present them in the most flattering light, but, almost involuntarily, the many rabbinic traditions collected in the vast repository of the Talmud nevertheless reveal the extent to which opinions varied. A popular story has the rabbinic leader Yohanan ben Zakkai fleeing Jerusalem at the height of the siege in order to request that the Romans give him the town of Yavneh as the place where he and his pupils could continue studying the Torah. The implication is that Judaism was thus saved, even though the Temple was destroyed, because the rabbis were, above all, religious teachers, apolitical and opposed to dangerous nationalist delusions.

But the earliest sources suggest that Yohanan ben Zakkai actually supported the war against the Romans until its doomed outcome was obvious. The even greater disaster of the Bar Kochba revolt sixty years later revealed still more starkly the split among rabbis. In 132, Simeon bar Kosba, nicknamed Bar Kochba (son of the star), led an uprising against the emperor, Hadrian. He was initially successful, but the Roman counter-attack inflicted devastating damage. Bar Kochba and his remaining followers died when Betar, their last stronghold, was stormed. As a result of the failed revolt Judea was left desolate, and Hadrian ordered that a harrow was to be drawn over Jerusalem and a new city, Aelia Capitolina, built on its site. Yet several leading rabbis of the time, including the illustrious Rabbi Akiva, had endorsed Bar Kochba, going so far as to call him the Messiah and encouraging their students to take up arms. Such fevered involvement in Messianism does not suggest that the rabbinic party had entirely forsaken politics for the studious life.

Similarly, the Talmud records an interesting exchange between Rabbi Judah ben Ilai, favourably treated by the Romans for his moderate views, and Rabbi Simeon ben Yohai, a supporter of Bar Kochba and forced into hiding because of his seditious opinions. Rabbi Judah praises the Romans: 'How beautiful are the deeds of that nation. They set up marketplaces, build bridges, construct baths.' Rabbi Simeon retorts: 'Everything they do is for their own good. They set up marketplaces to put their harlots there, baths for their pleasures, bridges to levy tolls.' There speaks the instantly recognisable voice of the revolutionary, terrorist, freedom fighter (depending on your point of view) down the ages.[1]

It took the crushing of the Bar Kochba rebellion (during which, according to the later Roman historian Dio Cassius, 50 fortresses and 985 settlements were razed and 580,000 Jews were killed) to finally convince the rabbinic authorities that they had to adopt a more placatory approach to Roman rule. The aphorism attributed to Haninah (probably it should be Hananiah), prefect of the priests, 'Pray for the welfare of the ruling power, for, were it not for fear of the government, men would swallow up each other alive', reflects the sardonic realism with which the rabbis came to terms with national defeat and adjusted accordingly to Roman authority post-135 in order to reinforce their own role as the new custodians of the Jewish people and religion.

It is indicative of their changed approach that a measure of Jewish autonomy was speedily restored, despite the bitterness engendered on both sides by the Bar Kochba revolt. A period of peaceful cooperation with the authorities followed. The accession of a conciliatory Roman emperor, Antonius Pius, in 138 helped the healing process. The *nasi* of the Sanhedrin was confirmed as patriarch of the Jews and given the right to collect taxes for Jewish institutions, to appoint judges for the Jewish courts and to send official delegates to Diaspora communities, where the majority of Jews lived. In return, these communities showed their respect to the memory of the Temple by offering financial support to the patriarchate. Under Judah the Prince (see chapter 1, page 9), who spoke both Hebrew and Greek in his household, in 212 the emperor, Caracalla, even extended Roman citizenship to Jews and most other peoples of the empire, admittedly as a bait for raising revenue, but symptomatic of the cordiality which now characterised rabbinic–Roman relations.

According to the contemporary and not unfriendly Church Father Origen, the patriarch was virtually as powerful as the former Judean kings, on occasion even passing the death penalty with Rome's tacit consent. He was guarded by a troop of German mercenaries, and the opulence of his court in Tiberias occasioned criticism from some colleagues.

Due to Roman sanction and underpinning, Rabbinic Judaism established itself as the sole Jewish political authority, functioning as a quasi-autonomous local government within the empire. In these favourable circumstances, it was able to consolidate its control and lay the foundations of the legal and communal framework that would order Jewish life throughout the Middle Ages, long after the Roman Empire had disappeared and Jews had come under the rule of Christianity and Islam.

Jewish life in Palestine ebbed and flowed according to the vicissitudes of the Roman Empire. Between 235 and 285, the empire was close to collapse, as barbarians threatened it from the north and the Persians from the east, and rival generals struggled for power. Heavy taxation and grim economic conditions in Galilee induced many Jews to emigrate. The steady spread of Christianity was given formal ratification by Constantine the Great, who granted official toleration to the religion, legalised clerical privileges and in 325 convened a Church council at Nicea to resolve doctrinal differences. His government moved to Byzantium, renamed Constantinople, and henceforth Palestine was administered from the eastern capital.

There was a marked increase in anti-Jewish legislation as a result of Christianity's triumph, and Judaism was reduced to a position of permanent, legal inferiority. The scope of the

Sanhedrin was further reduced in 399 when Honorius, emperor of the West, forbade the collection of the voluntary levy that hitherto had helped to maintain the patriarchate. Finally, when the patriarch, Gamaliel VI, died in 425 without male heir, Theodosius II abolished the office.

Briefly, when the Persians invaded Palestine during the reign of Heraclius, the Jews rose up against their Christian masters but paid dearly for their rebellion once Christianity was re-established in 628 CE. The sweeping conquests of Islam shortly afterwards, with Egypt, Syria and Palestine falling to Arab invaders, ushered in a new regime, though it made little appreciable difference to the remaining Jews. Their position had been in steady decline since the abolition of the patriarchate two hundred years previously. Whether in the ancient homeland or in the larger and more prosperous communities of the Diaspora, the tenor of Jewish life was now fixed, as it would remain for the next thirteen hundred years. The Jews had to learn to adapt to minority status wherever they lived. Powerlessness would be their defining characteristic. New stratagems for survival would be needed.

6 THE SHIFTING GROUND OF DIASPORA EXISTENCE

In simplified form, we have sketched fifteen hundred years of Jewish political history, roughly from the heyday of King David to the abolition of the Patriarchate. It is a cautionary tale of growth and decline, good and bad government, brief interludes of independence interspersed with long periods of subjugation by powerful empires. No doubt a similar tale could be told about the Phoenicians, the Assyrians, the Babylonians or any other ancient Near Eastern people that briefly came to notice then passed from history for ever.

That the Jews survived, and that their religion of Judaism as a distinctive civilisation has comfortably outlived the Greek, Roman, Persian and Ottoman Empires to which they once paid allegiance, was due in large part to the widespread dissemination and universal application of the Torah (Law) which governed the conduct of *all* Jews wherever they resided. Bound together and instantly recognisable by their practices, it could further be argued that for the Jews exile and dispersion, far from being the disasters they were invariably considered to be, were in fact blessings in disguise, enabling them to escape the fate that befell other contemporary nations rooted in a single territory. No mediaeval scholar or poet, adopting a conventional melancholy pose, would have dared to interpret languishing in the West while his heart was in the East as anything but divine punishment for Israel's sins. It was not until the emergence of the Reform movement at the beginning of the nineteenth century that nostalgia for the ancient homeland, and prayers for the restoration of the Temple and animal sacrifice, were positively rejected and the Diaspora experience was recast as the divine plan to enable Judaism to fulfil its mission as a light unto the nations.

The theological explanation for exile and the Messianic yearning for return went unchallenged for almost two millennia precisely because it was the tenets of Rabbinic Judaism that guided and controlled Jewish life, East and West, for all of that time. From the destruction of the Temple in 70 CE until the French Revolution, generations of rabbis were the de facto Jewish rulers. Already, by the time of Judah the Prince, the rabbis had legitimised their own status by inventing a historically fictitious 'chain of tradition' that traced their authority in a direct line via the prophets all the way back to Moses himself, 'our teacher'. Significantly, this hereditary line omits entirely the names of any of the kings or priests who led the people during the First and Second Temple periods. The rabbis were the new guardians of the faith, as much as the pope or the Holy Roman emperor would be for their constituencies in centuries to come.

The traditional process of rabbinic ordination, *semichah* (laying on [of hands]), ceased once the Palestinian patriarchate fell into desuetude and was not revived until the fourteenth century – and then in palely imitative form. Nevertheless, mediaeval rabbinic leaders still stressed their lineage and thereby imposed their authority over the community. In Babylonia, by far the largest centre of Jewish settlement after the failed revolts against Rome, the exilarch imaginatively claimed descent from the Judean kings originally taken into captivity by Nebuchadnezzar. His colleagues received the title *rav* instead of the now-defunct 'rabbi'.

Centuries later, the communal leader in Spain and North Africa under Islam, known as the *nagid*, could claim neither royal descent nor especially learned pedigree. Usually he acquired the post through being either a helpful financier at court or a royal physician. Even so, his office was invested with mythical origins in the legend of four emissaries from Babylonia who had come to the West to spread the learning of the rabbinical academies there. After the reintroduction of ordination, mediaeval rabbis had no qualms about linking themselves to the chain of tradition, as though it had never been severed. 'Every rabbi and legal expert has been ordained a rabbi by a preceding rabbi all the way back to Moses our teacher…and no householder may in any way question the words of the rabbi,' runs one Spanish text of the time.[1]

The nature of Jewish communal autonomy varied from country to country and from East to West. Contributory factors were the strength or weakness of central government, the tolerance or hostility of individual rulers, the economic importance of their Jewish subjects and the extent to which religious ideology underpinned policy. But it would be a mistaken simplification to characterise the Jews of the Middle Ages as a pariah people always living on the margins of society. In both the Muslim and Christian worlds, they occupied shifting ground, sometimes close to the centres of power, at other times powerless to defend themselves against mass movements such as the First Crusade, the Berber invasion of Spain by the Almohades in 1146 or popular uprisings in reaction to the plague of the Black Death.

The determining *religious* difference between the treatment of Jews under Islamic rule and their treatment under Christianity in Europe lay in the fact that, for Islam, Jews and Christians were both 'People of the Book' and therefore accorded formal, protected (*dhimmi*) status, whereas, for Christianity, the Jews had committed deicide and rejected the true redeemer, their downtrodden condition witness to the new covenant with Christianity. Under Islam, the so-called Pact of Omar (c. 800 CE) regulated association between Muslims and their *dhimmi* communities. Jews were permitted to retain and practise their religion, to appoint their own religious leaders and be guided by their own laws and customs. In return for this protection, they paid a poll tax (*jizya*) and were forbidden to build synagogues or houses higher than those of their Muslim neighbours, to bear arms or ride horses. The last two prohibitions came to be honoured more in the breach than the observance. By modern standards this amounted to second-class citizenship, but no such legalised tolerance existed in Christendom, where treatment varied according to the exigencies of time and place and the disposition of the ruler, and forced conversion, persecution or expulsion was a recurring feature.

In territories now under Islamic rule, leadership was exercised by the Babylonian exilarch, recognised by the caliphate as the Jewish representative, in conjunction with the presidents (*geonim*) of the two great rabbinic academies of Sura and Pumpedita. Their authority in all matters of Jewish law extended far beyond Arab lands to Diaspora communities elsewhere, but their system of religious control perpetuated itself through a small, fixed caste. Leadership was confined to half a dozen distinguished families. Jealously guarded privileges provoked resentment and opposition. A sustained attack against rabbinic hegemony was led by the dissident sect of the Karaites.

The greatest of the *geonim*, Egyptian-born Saadiah ben Joseph (882–942 CE), headed the counter-offensive against Karaism, and helped to restore rabbinic authority. The leadership of the *geonim* survived until the eleventh century, and the office of exilarch was maintained for a further two hundred years. By now, the Islamic empire had broken up into a number of smaller states. Religious and intellectual pre-eminence passed to a new setting for mediaeval Jewish culture: Muslim Spain.

Spain became an independent Muslim state in the latter half of the eighth century. Its population was a heterogeneous mix of races and religions – Arabs, Berbers, Visigoths, Christians and Jews. Toleration of ethnic minorities was a necessary plank of governance. The Jews, with links to co-religionists in other parts of the world, their knowledge of languages and their commercial acumen, were a valued element in society. They rose to positions of prominence at court, became landowning farmers and followed careers in medicine and astronomy. Their situation particularly fitted them for missions of diplomacy; ambiguity, discretion and reserve were essential characteristics for anyone wishing to prosper in alien surroundings.

Chasdai ibn Shaprut (c. 915–970) was a spectacular, but by no means unique, example of how high Jews could reach. Born into a wealthy family, Chasdai acquired in his youth a thorough knowledge of Arabic, Hebrew and Latin, the last usually the preserve only of the higher clergy. He also studied medicine and was appointed physician to caliph ‘Abd al-

Rahman of Cordova. Of easy charm, ability and probity, Chasdai became his master's trusted confidant and counsellor. Effectively, if unofficially, he was Cordova's minister of foreign affairs, as well as customs and excise officer for the port. It was to him that envoys presented their credentials. A by-product of his diplomatic involvement was the gift from the Byzantine emperor Constantine VII of a magnificent codex of Dioscorides' important work on botany, which Chasdai helped to translate into Arabic, thereby making it available to Arab and European science.

Chasdai's negotiating finesse was such that a member of a delegation from the German emperor Otto I wrote that he had 'never seen a man of such subtle intellect as the Jew ...'[2] His most famous diplomatic triumph was to persuade the Christian queen of Navarre to journey to Cordova with her son and grandson and there to prostrate herself before her old enemy, the Umayyad caliph, in order to implore his military aid against the kingdom of Leon. Chasdai vanquished her, according to a contemporary Jewish versifier, 'by the charm of his words, the strength of his wisdom, the force of his cunning and his thousand tricks'.

It was a measure not only of his rounded personality but also of the uninhibited manner in which Jews of the time moved between the public sphere and private religious observance that Chasdai was also leader of the Jewish community in Cordova and a major benefactor. Due to him, while maintaining cordial relations with the exilarch and Babylonian scholars, Spanish Jewry was able to assert its independence from Baghdad and embark upon the richest period of Andalusian Jewish culture. He encouraged study by importing Hebrew books from the East and gathering Jewish intellectuals around him. Poetry and scholarship flourished.

Born in Cordova three years after Chasdai died, Samuel ha-Nagid (993–1056) would win still greater renown. His rapid rise to authority and his political and military career represented the zenith of Jewish achievement in mediaeval Muslim Spain. In 1013, after a civil war and the conquest of Cordova by the Berber chieftain Sulaiman, many Jews emigrated to less turbulent principalities in the peninsula. Samuel and his family settled in Malaga, in the territory of Granada. There, his skill in Arabic calligraphy soon brought him to notice, and he was employed as secretary to the vizier. On the latter's death, the caliph of Granada appointed Samuel to the post and entrusted him with conduct of his diplomatic and military policy. Samuel became a leading figure at court and took a calculated gamble in 1037 by backing the elder brother, Badis, in a power struggle to assume the caliphate, although the majority of the nobles and several influential Jews had thrown their weight behind the younger son. Vindicated by events, Samuel not only retained his former position but was given command of the army as well. For nearly twenty years, until his death, Samuel was constantly in the field and was, if not the only, then certainly the most famous and successful Jewish general between the era of the Maccabees and the establishment of the State of Israel in 1948.

He was also a scholar and a poet. His command of Talmudic sources was such that he compiled a major compendium of rabbinic and *geonic* legal judgements, written in Hebrew, Aramaic and Arabic, which directly influenced later Spanish authorities. As a diverse and skilled poet in a society which prized literary composition as the mark of an educated person, he wrote of military campaigns, love, friendship and the vanities of human life. There have been few more succinct comments on the ravages of warfare than his four-line Hebrew poem: 'War is at first like a beautiful girl/with whom all men long to play/but in the end like a repulsive hag/whose suitors all weep and ache.' His protégé, Solomon ibn Gabirol, one of the greatest Hebrew poets of all time, dedicated several poems to him with the acknowledgement 'My father, my rider, my chariot'.[3]

As the illustrious de facto leader of Spanish Jewry, Samuel was the first to be accorded the title of *nagid* (prince). His son, Yehosef, succeeded him as vizier and commander, while able contemporaries served the courts of Seville, Saragossa, Cordova, Toledo and other cities. Despite the illustration of how high Jews could reach in Muslim society, it has to be admitted that the good times did not last. In 1086 the Almoravides, Berber fanatics from North Africa, poured into the peninsula to help their Muslim co-religionists stem the advance of the northern, Christian kingdoms. The victorious Almoravide rulers dismissed Jews from all positions of authority and imposed heavy fines on the wealthy community of Lucena in an attempt to force a massed conversion to Islam.

Almost a century later, other Berber tribes, from the Atlas region of Morocco, crossed the straits to do battle with Christianity. The Almohades were uncompromising fundamentalists. They instituted a systematic persecution of Christians and Jews. The choice was forced conversion or expulsion. Some Jews converted publicly but continued to practise their religion secretly; others took to the roads leading north and found temporary haven in Christian Spain, where they were welcomed as valuable immigrants.

By 1172, all of Muslim Spain was ruled by the Almohad dynasty. It is a moot point whether reactionary religious forces are a response to economic decline or a symptom of it. Italian maritime cities now dominated the Mediterranean trade routes, squeezing the international mercantile class in Muslim countries. It was now, as an act of protectionism, that the Almohades tried to revive the defunct Pact of Omar in order to regulate the commercial activities of religious minorities. The bulk of Iberian and North African Jewry became steadily poorer under the Almohades. By the time they were forced out of Spain by the alliance of Christian Spain, Portugal and Navarre, whose armies inflicted a crushing defeat at the battle of Los Navas de Toloso in 1212, the Almohades' harsh policy had ensured that not a single, professing Jew remained in the south of the country.

Most of them, an estimated 200,000, lived in Castile, Aragon and Portugal, enjoying under Christian kings the favoured status that had formerly been theirs under Muslim caliphs. The Christian reconquest of the peninsula did not noticeably affect their standing or that of Muslims. For almost two centuries, the three faiths coexisted amicably. Jews rose to positions of importance at northern courts as previously they had done in the Muslim south. Diplomacy and finance were their usual avenues of preferment. Samuel Abulafia (c. 1320–1361) became chief treasurer to Pedro the Cruel of Castile. Under his stewardship, several synagogues were built for the three hundred-odd Jewish communities of the realm, including the lovely Sinagoga del Transito in Toledo, where much of the former *juderia* still stands as poignant testimony to a once-flourishing and confident community.

Charters defined the status of the Spanish–Jewish communities, guaranteeing their economic and religious rights. Jews participated in the professions and crafts, with their own craft guilds and guildhalls in the larger cities. These *aljamas*, as the Spanish communities were called, were sizeable organisations, and the different social classes lobbied for representation on the committees responsible for education, the legal system and charity.

Intellectual life was vigorous. The natural sciences, astronomy, mathematics, medicine and philosophy were studied, influenced by Muslim thought. The Talmudic scholarship of northern Europe made its way to Spain as Ashkenazi Jews sought refuge from persecution in Germany and the Rhineland. Several Jews became major landowners, as the Christian kings completed the reconquest of the peninsula and sold off large tracts for development.

An inscription in the Toledo synagogue attesting to the high standing of Samuel Abulafia concludes, 'since the day of our Exile, no son of Israel has attained to such exalted estate.' The reference to the great dispersions of 586 BCE and 70 CE was no mere religious piety but recognition of contemporary realities. In Spain, under Muslim caliphs or Christian kings, as with Judea under Babylonian or Roman rule, maintaining the balance between conflicting and more powerful forces required infinite tact and subtle calculation on the part of the Jewish leadership. If it miscalculated, the results could be catastrophic.

Such catastrophe happened in 1366, when civil war broke out between Pedro the Cruel and his half-brother, Henry of Trastanara. Discontent had been simmering for years. Henry's followers united under the slogan of liberating the country from a tyrannical ruler. In 1360 or 1361 (the date is uncertain), Samuel Abulafia was suddenly arrested, tortured and thrown into prison, where he died. The reasons why are unknown, but it is plausible to speculate that enemies at court had accused him of clandestine support for Henry, even though Pedro was dismissively known as 'king of the Jews' and Abulafia had been zealous in protecting his royal interests.

Both sides called in foreign troops, English and French, the Black Prince commanding the British soldiery, who fought for Pedro, and Bertrand de Guesclin taking charge of Henry's mercenaries. In the accompanying propaganda war, Henry's supporters blamed Pedro's 'foreign' advisers – a euphemism for Jews – for all of Castile's misfortunes and demanded their dismissal.

Certainly, the Jews suffered from the depredations of both sides. Thousands died in the communities of Burgos and Toledo, which had declared for Pedro, and the survivors were forced to pay swingeing tribute. Pedro, for his part, allowed Muslim fighters from Granada to seize the three hundred Jewish families of Jaen and sell them into slavery.

Significantly, though, once Henry became the sole, acknowledged king after Pedro was killed in battle in March 1369 he reverted to the well-tried formula of taking the Jews under his official protection and confirming their privileges. During his reign, as with his predecessors, Jews were prominent in organising government finances and acting as tax farmers. In return, they affirmed their loyalty to the new regime. A contemporary writer answered anti-Jewish slurs by protesting, '…our lives and welfare depend upon the well-being of the state under whose government we live…Far be it from us to curse our kings, for they are a shield and a buckler and a refuge unto us…'[4]

But it is a recurring historical phenomenon that hardline zealotry follows in the wake of religious victories. The Church in Spain was no exception, demanding ever-tougher legislation against Jews and Muslims as the reconquest established its hold over more of the country. Social, religious and political unrest had spread throughout Europe in the aftermath of the Black Death, and in their sermons priests were not slow to find handy scapegoats. In 1391, anti-Jewish violence erupted in Seville and spread throughout Castile and Aragon. Thousands were slaughtered by rampaging mobs, which indiscriminately attacked Christian homes and property as well.

Spanish Jewry was traumatised. Tens of thousands converted en masse to Christianity, led by the wealthiest and most prominent members of the community. This mass apostasy encouraged the Church, the Dominican order in the vanguard, to put extra pressure on remaining Jews to become *conversos*. Punitive legislation and constant harassment had a draining effect. Within twenty-five years, these 'new Christians' had become almost as large a group as loyal Jews, being rewarded for their conversions by becoming bishops and Church officials, marrying into the nobility, even the Aragonese royal family, and entering branches of the state administration that had recently been barred to them. Temporarily, it *paid* to become a Christian.

But the popularity of these *conversos* did not last. They were accused of secretly practising their former religion, and in 1449 an anti-*converso* riot broke out in Toledo, the first of several over the next thirty years. The marriage of Ferdinand and Isabella in 1479, which united the kingdoms of Aragon and Castile, worsened the situation for converted Jews. A year later, the Inquisition was established to root out heretics. The first auto-da-fé was held early in 1481, when six men and women of Jewish extraction were burnt alive. Under its most fearsome Inquisitor-General, Fra Tomas de Torquemada (ironically of Jewish descent), the Inquisition confiscated the property of some 30,000 allegedly secret Jews and burnt at the stake those who did not repent satisfactorily. It should be remembered, though, that initially the Inquisition was set up to investigate suspicious *conversos*, not openly professing Jews.

The distinction soon blurred. In 1492, a fabricated blood-libel charge at Avila was the pretext that allowed Ferdinand and Isabella to issue, from the newly captured Alhambra of Granada (the last Muslim stronghold on the Iberian peninsula), a decree expelling all Jews from Spanish dominions. It was argued that this would protect genuine *conversos* from the surreptitious influence of their former co-religionists. The Jews were given four months to leave.

Illustrating the complex, entwined and enduring nature of the Jewish–Christian symbiosis in Spain, even when obdurate religious principle was winning out at the expense of pragmatic self-interest, it was an eminent Jewish advisor at court, Don Isaac Abravanel, who pleaded unsuccessfully with his royal masters to have the decree rescinded. He had fled to Spain, after serving as treasurer to the king of Portugal, to escape a conspiracy charge. When his protestations failed, he accompanied many of his fellow exiles to Italy, where he found employment at the court of Naples before finally settling in Venice. In all, between 100,000 and 150,000 Jews were forced out of Spain in the summer of 1492, bidding farewell to a territory they had called home for over one thousand years and where Jewish culture had achieved its most brilliant synthesis to date of rabbinic learning and secular attainment.

Subsequent generations likened the expulsion from Spain to the exiles of 586 BCE and 70 CE, even claiming (erroneously) that the three catastrophes shared the same date in the Jewish calendar. Creating a neat symmetry of suffering overlooked the fundamental reality of three vastly differing contexts. All that 586 BCE, 70 and 1492 had in common was the end result. The First Temple was destroyed because of political miscalculation – choosing the wrong alliances. The fall of the Second Temple was due, in large part, to internal discord – 'groundless hatred', in the phrase of the rabbis. The expulsion from Spain came about because, despite their influence with and commercial usefulness to both religions, the Jews were squeezed remorselessly in the fight for supremacy between Christianity and Islam. Whether precariously independent in 586, a vassal outpost of empire in 70 or a discrete religious minority in 1492, the Jews could not avoid the fate that befell all small, vulnerable peoples in the ancient and mediaeval world. They were at the whim of larger, more powerful forces. To endure at all in such circumstances was a remarkable achievement and vindication of the pragmatic, relativist approach to survival – cutting one's coat according to the cloth.

7 FACTORS IN SURVIVAL

Broadly speaking, the Jewish people are divided between those of Sephardic descent, a generic description (from Obadiah 1:20) for Jews who lived under Islam in Spain and the East, and Ashkenazim (from Genesis 10:3), who spread through Christian Europe in the wake of the Roman Empire's decline and fall. The customary generalisation is to see the Jewish experience in the East as generally benign, if humiliating, at least until the disruptive advent of Zionism, whereas life in the West, at least until the dawn of the Enlightenment, was harsh and downtrodden, regularly punctuated by pogroms, persecution and expulsions.

For those who want it, there is enough evidence to justify such a bleak conclusion, but it is hardly the whole picture. Certainly, unlike Islam, the response of Christian rulers to the Jews in their midst had the added piquancy of theological animus, as well as its usual financial and commercial considerations. But European Jewish history is regional, depending upon where on the continent Jews settled. As each regional community had its own distinctive character, its own rites and customs, its own autonomous self-government and its own utility to the ruling powers, the fortunes of each ebbed and flowed according to the larger religious and national forces that were shaping European history and sucking up every ethnic minority, not just the Jews, in their current.

For example, once the barbarian invasions had been halted, Jewish immigration was consistently encouraged by the Carolingian dynasty. Jewish merchants received favoured treatment because of their trade connections with the Mediterranean and further east. From their bases in France, others set forth on daunting missions across Eastern Europe and over the Russian steppes to the Middle East, sometimes continuing as far as India and China. Throughout the tenth and eleventh centuries, Jewish businessmen were the familiars of Western Europe's kings and nobles, who blithely disregarded the canonical restrictions imposed by successive Church councils on Jews, such was their economic value. In the Rhineland, local rulers invited them in. As a consequence, Jewish settlers came to Mainz, Worms, Speyer (where the bishop defended his Jews against the knights of the First Crusade), Cologne and other burgeoning German cities.

The communities that sprang up were independent and self-regulating, with no equivalent of the exilarch or *nagid* to represent them at court. Each *kahal*, as the community was called, set up its own law court, enacted its own regulations and controlled the behaviour of its residents, much as local barons and warlords governed feudal Christendom.

Mediaeval society was hierarchical yet fluid in composition, built upon complex and overlapping relationships of loyalty and privilege, with kings, nobles and clergy competing to extend their own spheres of influence. The notion of the sovereign state, in the sense of political power being located exclusively in a central authority, simply did not exist in the Middle Ages. Instead, each class or grouping within society looked to ally itself with a powerful overlord who would offer corporate privileges as the quid pro quo for fealty; only the poor serf tied to the land had nothing to bargain with.

The Jews, typically urban dwellers and adept at cultivating judicious alliances, usually received the same privileges as burghers, foremost among which was freedom of movement, an essential for those engaged in commerce. They played their part in the life of the city, sometimes occupying municipal office as a representative of their craft or guild, sometimes fighting in the city's defence. A fifteenth-century Italian jurist defined the civic status of Jews as follows: 'Jews are considered to be of the same people and of the [corporate] body of the same city, although they may not be considered members of the same spiritual body.'[1]

It could be fairly argued that privileges, however favourable, are not the same as rights. The notion of privilege presupposes someone who grants it and therefore could also withdraw or redefine it, as frequently happened to Jews throughout the Middle Ages. In that sense, it is a precarious gift, and excluded European Jews from a citizen's due expectations or even their formal status as legally enshrined under Islam. But it must be emphasised that *no* individual in the pre-modern state was guaranteed 'rights'. The concept of reciprocal obligations between the state and the subject was centuries away. Within the stratified and subtly graded layers of mediaeval European society, it was a case of survival of the fittest and devil take the hindmost.

It was as if historical experience had adapted the Jews for survival. The very fact that they enjoyed royal and papal protection is testimony to their successful assimilation within the mediaeval hierarchy. Successive popes, starting with Calixtus II (1119–1124), confirmed the right of Jews to practise their religion and be protected from violence while forbidding them to exercise authority over Christians or convert them. Whichever aspect of this policy was emphasised at any given time depended upon its cultural and Christian context. The Jews of Rome, therefore, enjoyed a period of tolerant well-being under Renaissance popes, while the hostile spirit of the Counter-Reformation provoked a negative reaction that instituted the ghetto system.

Similarly, in 1103 the German emperor Henry IV, mindful of the Crusader rampages of 1096, extended to Jews living in his territories the same royal protection granted to priests, monks, merchants, widows, orphans and virgins. Again, the wider context is relevant. Reports from pilgrims to Palestine about Muslim desecration of the holy places had inflamed Christianity. In response, the First Crusade was an extended pillage from Metz to Jerusalem, where in 1097 Godfrey de Bouillon's army fought its way into the city, herded all the Jews into a synagogue and set it on fire. Both the Church and secular rulers were shocked by the indiscriminate mob violence and took steps to ensure that the Second Crusade in 1146 was more tightly controlled. Granting Jews the status of *servi camerae nostri* (serfs of the royal chamber, i.e. the emperor's property) might seem to betoken degradation, but in fact it afforded them special protection.

Such measures highlighted the vulnerability of Jewish communities and other minorities in an overwhelmingly Christian environment. The interplay of religious and economic factors would determine the treatment of Jews throughout the late Middle Ages. A money economy was developing in Europe at a time when the Church taught that usury was theologically repugnant. The Jew, standing outside the legal jurisdiction of the Church, could readily answer the great demand for loans with his liquid assets amassed from mercantile connections. Although other groups, such as Lombard bankers, the Cahorsins and the Templars, were given dispensation to lend money, Jews dominated the occupation, often with the connivance of their noble protectors, who shared in the profits. When royal treasuries could no longer support their debts, as happened in France in 1182, or the arrival of Italian banking firms rendered Jewish moneylenders superfluous, as happened in England in 1290, the Jews were summarily expelled, their property and assets reverting to the king.

The twin forces of mammon and religion coalesced in 1348 with the outbreak of the Black Death. Jews, probably because of their hygienic and dietary practices, suffered less than their neighbours from the bubonic plague that carried off a third of Europe's population. The credulous masses gave ear to the charge that Jews had poisoned the wells, just as they shivered at the thought of Christian children being murdered at Passover for their blood to be used in baking unleavened bread. Pope Clement VI issued a bull condemning the libel and ordering the Jews to be protected, to little avail. Christian trade guilds diverted their traditional hostility towards the lesser nobility and other classes onto the Jewish financiers who sustained them, and it was a fortuitous opportunity for debtors to attack their creditors. From southern France to northern Germany, hardly a Jewish community was spared. Christian flagellants further incited the mobs. In Germany alone, 60 large and 150 small communities were destroyed.

Without meaning to minimise the reality of Jewish suffering in the late Middle Ages, it must be pointed out that it was a reflection of the war, plague, social breakdown, economic stagnation, religious superstition and abiding insecurity that affected all of feudal European society. Anyone who has read Chaucer or seen Ingmar Bergman's film *The Seventh Seal* will have an inkling of how poor, nasty, brutish and short life was for everyone, from the lord in his castle to the serf in his hovel, with the continual fear and danger of violent death.

The distinctive Jewish garb or markings worn at different times in mediaeval society should be judged in the same light. At least some of the Jewish dress in the Middle Ages, such as the hat, originated out of choice, not compulsion. The plethora of corporations, guilds, crafts and religious orders each wore its own distinguishing uniform to symbolise group differences. Similarly, the yellow patch or star, associated for ever with the Nazi genocide of European Jewry, originated under Islam to demonstrate publicly that its wearers enjoyed official protection. One fourteenth-century Egyptian writer compared its efficacy to that of an amulet.

Whenever the system of local protection for Jews broke down catastrophically, as it did during the First Crusade and the Black Death, it was due to popular, anti-establishment uprisings, fuelled by religiously inspired Judeophobia that the authorities were powerless to stem. Where central government was strong, the Jews could rely on a fair degree of security. Where it was fragmented, as in Germany, they were at the arbitrary whim of circumstances and subject to attack or expulsion. That is why the 1492 exile from Spain was unique and should not be classified as the climax of a melancholy litany of persecutions, such as the expulsions from England and France, the Rindfleisch massacres of 1298 or those of

1348–1349 after the Black Death. In Spain, the reconquest had united Church and monarchy in an absolutist Christian state. Elsewhere in Europe, temporal and spiritual power were acrimoniously disengaging and drawing the lines between Caesar's jurisdiction and God's. That is why, whenever Jews were driven out of one principality, another would be willing to welcome their talents and commercial value, whatever Church teachings might say about them.

Unless these abrupt reversals of Jewish fortune are viewed as side effects of the wider upheavals whereby the European nation state was struggling to emerge, with power slowly becoming concentrated in the hands of a sovereign at the expense of the vested interests of nobles, clergy and corporations, it is not possible to understand why at some times Jewish communities could enjoy autonomous privileges and quasi-free status and at others be singled out for religious victimisation, persecution and expulsion. During the Middle Ages, it worked to Jewish advantage that the Church, kings and nobility were factionalised and jealously protected their special interests. But, as government coalesced around the central figure of a sovereign, it was inevitable that the privileges previously enjoyed by favoured castes within society, including the Jews, would be whittled away.

Poland provides an illustrative study of this process at work. Just as, from the ninth to the eleventh centuries, Jews had been drawn to France and the Rhineland in order to fill an economic vacuum, so too was Poland a similar magnet to Jews (and Christians) from Germany from the thirteenth to the sixteenth centuries. In order to encourage immigration to sparsely populated territories that had suffered from Tartar depredations, in 1264 Boleslav the Pious issued a model charter of liberties and protection for the Jews. Between 1334 and

1367, King Casimir the Great amplified the inducements, followed in similar fashion a few years later by the grand duke of Lithuania, so that large numbers of Ashkenazim settled in Eastern Europe.

As their forebears had done in Spain, the newcomers displayed vitality, acumen and adaptability in taking advantage of a tolerant milieu. They became intermediaries between the landed nobility and the peasants, acting as tax collectors and landlords' agents, importing textiles and luxury goods, exporting furs and raw materials and distributing merchandise and agricultural products. Their participation was essential at the great fairs around which Polish commercial life revolved.

Economic opportunity and physical security attracted waves of Jewish immigration. Between 1500 and 1648, Polish Jewry expanded from 10–15,000 residents to more than 150,000. They pioneered the colonisation of large tracts of the Ukraine, leasing estates from their absentee landlords and collecting taxes and produce from the serfs. It was the beginning of that unique phenomenon of Jewish rural domicile, the *shtetl* (small town). Hundreds of such hamlets spread out through Poland, the Ukraine, Galicia and Bessarabia, and survived all economic, social and military hardships until the twentieth century.

The reason why Polish–Jewish life prospered was two-fold. First, communities enjoyed the protection of successive kings and powerful nobles, whose agents they became. Second, for a good part of the sixteenth century, the bitterest religious dispute was between Catholicism and Reform, easing pressure on the Jews despite the prejudices of ignorant country priests and the economic jealousy of the peasantry. With a weak central government and ambitious nobles flexing their muscles against royal authority, a large measure of autonomy devolved upon the Jews.

As a result, Polish Jewry was able to organise itself into the most extensive and effective system of self-government that the Diaspora was ever to know, modelled on the regional and national parliaments of the Polish nobility. Each local *kehillah* (small community) appointed a committee of trustees that collected the government taxes and supervised educational and social requirements. The larger communities employed paid officials, including the rabbi and a *shtadlan* (intercessor) who spoke fluent Polish and represented the Jews before the king and in the law courts. It was not surprising, given such a propitious atmosphere, that rabbinic scholarship flourished as never since the heyday of Babylonian Jewry. Needy students were supported by public funds in scores of academies (*yeshivot*), where Talmudic and rabbinic texts were studied intensively.

The Council of the Four Lands (*Vaad Arba Aratzot*) was a national body composed of the leading rabbinic and lay figures of the four provinces of Great Poland, Little Poland, Podolia and Volhynia. It met twice a year, usually at the spring fair of Lublin and the summer fair of Jaroslaw, in order to coordinate all matters of Jewish concern, from apportioning the tax burden to choosing *shtadlanim* and issuing ordinances for local implementation. The Council maintained a virtual pressure group at the Polish parliament, causing a critic to claim, with polemical exaggeration, that 'in practice Jews do not let any law materialise which is unfavourable to them'. The tightly governed infrastructure of Polish–Lithuanian Jewry ensured that communal affairs functioned smoothly in tranquil times and, in the chaotic times that would shortly submerge Poland, it enabled the

Jews to survive a disaster which surely would otherwise have annihilated them.

In 1648, led by Bogdan Chmielnicki, Ukrainian Cossacks staged a nationalist revolt against Polish sovereignty. The Ukraine was a volatile religious and ethnic mix of Greek Orthodox peasants, Roman Catholic landlords, urban Jews and Cossacks. For two months of that summer, Chmielnicki's hordes roamed the countryside, indiscriminately slaughtering Jews, Poles, Catholics and Greek Orthodox Uniates (who recognised the pope).

Worse was to follow as warfare dragged on for twenty years, sucking in the Russians, who invaded north-eastern Poland and the Ukraine, and Charles X of Sweden, who advanced into western Poland. Massacre, famine and epidemics were visited upon Polish Jewry. At least a quarter of the community died, more than 50,000 men, women and children. The suffering was terrible, but it should be borne in mind, by way of grim perspective, that the religious wars of the seventeenth century involved the greatest uprooting of populations in Europe in the time between the barbarian invasions and the wars of the twentieth century.

Eventually, the Treaty of Andrusovo, signed in 1667, brought an end to the fighting and this period of Polish history, which was referred to with eloquent feeling in later textbooks as 'the Deluge'. The work of Jewish reconstruction began soon after, even in the Ukraine, the scene of the most terrible atrocities. But never again would Polish Jewry experience that happy blend of economic prosperity, relative physical security, effective protection and wide-ranging autonomy. In 1764, the Council of the Four Lands was finally abolished by the parliament of a partitioned Polish state, its purpose having been steadily eroded by interfering noblemen, the growing insubordination of an impoverished community and the government's wish to collect Jewish taxes directly.

The Polish lesson was clear and in luridly magnified detail reiterated the typical Diaspora experience elsewhere in Europe. Where central authority was strong, the Jews prospered and were safeguarded; where central authority was struggling to impose itself against competing interests, private protection was at best a transient blessing. It is a lesson that other religious and ethnic minorities have learnt to their cost in our day, from Africa to former Yugoslavia, and an uncomfortable one for liberals to digest, because it appears to teach that absolutism, hopefully benign, is the best model of government for protecting the well-being of minorities.

8 EMERGING FROM THE GHETTO

In the aftermath of the Deluge, Jews took to the highways of Europe, along with other refugees. Some wandered south into Moravia, Bohemia, Austria and Hungary, others continued on to Italy. Westwards, by way of Danzig and the Vistula region, Jewish fugitives came to newly independent Holland, where a sizeable *marrano* community was already settled in Amsterdam, a city whose most notorious erstwhile member, the philosopher Spinoza, was excommunicated for his heretical views in 1656.

In the main, though, they fled no further than they had to, back to Germany and those free cities and small principalities ready to admit Jews. The Thirty Years War, that mother and father of all wars of religion, had disastrous consequences in many respects but was strangely beneficial to the Jews. The decline of imperial authority and the resulting proliferation of petty states worked to Jewish advantage, as the refugees resettled in areas of a territory their ancestors had vacated three centuries earlier after the Black Death.

The German-speaking lands comprised more than one hundred independent states and mini-states, ranging in size from serious European powers such as Austria, Prussia, Saxony and Bavaria to miniature feudal principalities dotted around a nobleman's castle. Every tiny court, with its Protestant or Catholic prince in his imitative version of Versailles, required funding. A new kind of Jewish entrepreneur emerged as a result – the court Jew (*Hofjude*), whose commercial contacts with co-religionists in the north Atlantic ports, in Poland–Lithuania and along the Mediterranean could be summoned up on his patron's behalf. In return, these court Jews received a protected status for themselves and their families which was denied to the ghetto residents of Frankfurt, Worms, Hanover, Berlin and other cities. Whereas a typical ghetto Jew was required to pay a poll tax (*Liebzoll*), which was also levied on livestock, when he wished to travel from one vicinity to another, court Jews and their retainers dressed à la mode, aped the style of the nobility and had tutors to educate their children.

A characteristic and lucrative occupation of court Jews was as purveyor of supplies to the standing armies maintained by each principality. Samuel Oppenheimer (1630–1703), court Jew to the Austrian Hapsburgs, was succeeded by his nephew, Samson Wertheimer (1658–1724), who provisioned the imperial armies during the War of the Spanish Succession before being made chief rabbi of Hungary by Carl VI. Most flamboyant of all was Joseph Oppenheimer, known as the 'Jew Süss' (c. 1698–1738), who was appointed finance minister to the court of Wurttemberg in 1732. His monetary efficiency made him many enemies, who took their revenge after Duke Carl Alexander's death by accusing Oppenheimer of embezzlement and having sexual relations with Christian women. He was hanged in Stuttgart, having refused to save his life by being baptised. The German–Jewish novelist Lion Feuchtwanger wrote a book about Oppenheimer's career, which the Nazis distorted into a viciously anti-Semitic film.

At a superficial level, the fate of the Jew Süss appears to reiterate a constant lesson of Diaspora history – the precarious and transient nature of dependence on patronage. At a deeper level, these court Jews – and there were many lesser-known ones as well as those who merit a mention in encyclopaedias – represent a significant shift in the structures of authority within Jewish communal life. For the first time, there were Jewish individuals in wider society who did not necessarily speak for, lead or participate in their particular community. On occasion, their leadership might be imposed upon the community, as in the case of Samson Wertheimer, who, as it happens, was a conscientious and effective chief rabbi. At other times, they might use their influence to intercede on behalf of fellow Jews. But the internal organisation of *kahal* self-government, which had worked successfully throughout the Middle Ages, could no longer be taken for granted. An elite had emerged whose first loyalty was to their gentile ruler rather than the Jewish community. The first cracks were beginning to appear in a socio-religious structure that had done service for several hundred years of Diaspora existence but would be blown wide apart by the French Revolution at the end of the century.

This slow disintegration of a well-tried formula that had hitherto safeguarded limited Jewish autonomy was due to two paradoxically opposite causes; on the one hand, the growing strength of the absolutist state in Prussia and elsewhere, which concentrated power in the hands of the monarch at the expense of vested interests such as the nobility, corporations or religious foundations; and, on the other hand, the growing weakness of central government in a country such as Poland, where a collapsing economy led to widespread social anarchy that was reflected in the breakdown of the Jewish communal system.

Eking out a living in the countryside or in the towns, forced out of crafts and trades by the Catholic guilds, Poland's 750,000 Jews had little influence on the regional and national *kehillah* assemblies that nominally governed them. They resented the concentration of power in a few wealthy families, and accusations of unfair taxation and corruption were common. Their reaction was the standard one – a refusal to pay their taxes. No longer able to fulfil its prime task of collecting money from Jewish subjects and its authority dissolving in tandem with that of central government, the Council of the Four Lands was abolished in 1764, more than twenty years after the absolutist and atheist Frederick II (the Great) had formally declared that 'all religions must be tolerated. Every man may seek spiritual salvation in his own manner.'

Whether through the strength or the weakness of central government, the result was the same. European Jews were being detached from their traditional communal support structure. It is worth noting in this context that the swift rise of the *Chasidic* movement from the 1740s onwards was largely due to disaffection with the *kehillah* system and the rigidity of its rabbinic officers. As the bitterness intensified between the *Chasidim* and their opponents, the *Mitnaggedim*, a new phenomenon manifested itself: one side would denounce the other, not only internally, within the confines of the *kehillah*, but also externally, to the central authorities. A weak Jewish faction would look for support from a weak government.

Rabbinic Judaism was losing its power to be the sole regulating force in the lives of its followers.

At first, it was the fortunate few with economic leverage who could distance themselves from the community. The vast majority of Jews still lived in overcrowded ghettos, an impoverished urban proletariat subject to repressive legislation that was the legacy of the Reformation and the Catholic reaction to it. But the Age of Enlightenment was about to dawn. With it, the relationship between Jews and their countries of domicile would change for ever. As always in Diaspora history, it required a supple Jewish adaptation to changed circumstances.

The Enlightenment, with its ideals of tolerance, brotherhood and universalism, was famously defined by Immanuel Kant as the 'liberation of man from his self-incurred immaturity'. Spreading to Germany from England and France, the Enlightenment found fertile soil in Prussia, which the dramatist Gotthold Lessing had described as 'Europe's most enslaved country'. Organised Christianity was the symbol of all that was retrograde about societies which discouraged people from thinking for themselves. Espousing the cause of downtrodden and discriminated-against Jewry was one way of challenging the Church and its reactionary clerics, who were held responsible for many of the malaises of the *ancien régime*. Although the French Encyclopaedists were dismissive of *all* religion and Voltaire was personally antipathetic to Jews, the logic of their arguments about the social contract and individual freedom perforce had to apply to Jews as it did to other subjects of the state.

For their part, the Jewish middle classes responded avidly to the Enlightenment cult of *Bildung* (self-improvement through education). Christians and Jews would mingle in the literary and artistic salons of Berlin, where the grace, wit and brightness of the Jewish intelligentsia gave the lie to the assertion of the Christian theologian Johann Michaelis that 'a noble Jew was a poetic impossibility'. Moses Mendelssohn, the son of a poor scribe who won fame as an essayist and philosopher (the Jewish Socrates), was the embodiment of the *Bildung* ideal that non-Christians too could become people of refinement and learning if given the chance. A lifelong friend of Lessing, whose 1779 play *Nathan the Wise* was clearly based on him, Mendelssohn encouraged the historian Wilhelm Christian Dohm to write a pamphlet entitled *Concerning the Amelioration of the Civil Status of the Jews* in 1781. It sufficiently influenced the Austrian emperor, Joseph II, for him to issue a *Toleranzpatent* the following year that granted Austria's Jews wide commercial and domiciliary freedoms and annulled previous regulations that required married Jewish men to wear beards, forbade Jews to leave their homes before noon on Sundays and Christian holidays and barred them from public parks. Henceforth, business records were to be kept in German, not Yiddish, and Jewish children were to be encouraged to attend state schools. In 1787, the first Jewish recruits joined the Austrian army.

The *de haut en bas* concern of the Enlightenment to improve the lot of Jews was mirrored in the activities of its Jewish self-help equivalent, the *Haskalah* movement. Its exponents, the *maskilim* (enlighteners), sought to integrate well-educated, ethically aware, socially productive Jews into general society by combining the best of the Jewish cultural heritage with secular knowledge. Mendelssohn and his followers founded the *Freischule* in Berlin, which offered a general curriculum as well as Jewish subjects, then translated the Pentateuch into German and in 1783 published the first modern Jewish periodical, which was dedicated to a new aesthetic of Hebrew literature, morality and art.

Traditionalists feared, with good cause, that the primacy of Talmudic study would be overthrown in the clamour for *Bildung* and *Kultur*. In order to hasten the speed of Jewish emancipation, the richest, most successful, best-educated men and women chose to convert to Christianity. Although reliable statistics are not available, certainly the rate of conversion was far higher than at any time since some sixty per cent of Spanish Jewry converted in the fifteenth century. Growing toleration was succeeding where persistent persecution had failed. A rabbi in Breslau likened the wave of conversions to an 'earthquake' and a Lutheran pastor in Königsberg predicted that the entire Jewish community was about to disappear. While Mendelssohn himself remained devoutly observant until his death, four of his six children converted, along with an estimated half of Berlin's Jews.

In many, perhaps most, cases, converting was a calculated decision to better one's chances of social or professional advancement in a Christian society that was becoming increasingly sceptical about religion but still maintained the forms. That would explain why double the number of Jewish women than men converted between 1780 and 1840. They had nothing to gain from it politically or professionally in a pre-suffrage epoch, so presumably did so for marriage purposes. But, for Heinrich Heine and thousands of his talented contemporaries, the baptismal font was, in his wry flippancy, merely 'the entrance ticket to European culture'.

No doubt some converted for idealistic reasons, to further the Kantian goal of a universal religion. Certainly that was the motive behind the open letter that David Friedlander, a scholarly merchant prince and one of

Mendelssohn's confidants, sent to Wilhelm Teller, the foremost Protestant cleric in Berlin. Friedlander strongly disapproved of opportunistic conversions; his aim was to reform Judaism, not bury it. Nevertheless, in his letter he proposed that Jews would be ready to join the Lutheran Church if it could be done on the basis of shared moral values, without having to acknowledge the divinity of Christ or undergo baptism. He envisioned a rational Enlightenment faith practised in a tolerant secular state upholding freedom of conscience – a Unitarian church-synagogue, as it were. Nothing came of his proposal, but, nearly one hundred years later, Theodor Herzl, the founder of political Zionism, would suggest something similar in a playful sketch about how to solve the perennial Jewish Question.

Soon, the single most important event in modern history would render academic all the arguments of Jewish and Christian theorists about achieving emancipation. The French Revolution was about to break down the ghetto walls. Although European Jews were passive witnesses of the tumultuous events taking place in Paris, the French Revolution marked a turning point in Jewish history which was as decisive as the Babylonian exile, the destruction of the Second Temple or the expulsion from Spain. The 1789 Declaration of the Rights of Man, proclaiming that 'all men are born, and remain, free and equal in rights', catapulted the Jew into the modern world.

The debates in the French National Assembly about whether or not the Declaration of Rights extended to Jews too had been among that body's longest and stormiest, a perfect illustration of Enlightenment stereotypes and well-meaning concerns. The clerical opposition insisted that the Jews were a deicide nation governed by barbarous laws that precluded them from full citizenship. Delegates from Alsace accused the Jews of exploiting the peasantry. Robespierre and other advocates of Jewish emancipation conceded that they were indeed a degraded people, though the victims of others' vices, and could be regenerated through incorporation in the body politic. Finally, the Parisian deputy Clermont-Tonnerre proposed the solution in a famous formula: 'Everything for the Jews as citizens, nothing as a nation.'

Mendelssohn had advised his fellow Jews to 'adopt the habits and constitution of the land in which you live but retain the religion of your forefathers'. Using that as their doctrine, the *maskilim* gave a radical new interpretation to the ancient dictum, 'the law of the state is the law'. Ever since Samuel had first formulated the principle in third-century Babylonia, it had been understood to cede certain civil powers, such as collecting taxes, to the state, in return for which Jewish religious law remained autonomous. As Napoleon's armies conquered northern Europe, the *maskilim*, who, in accord with Enlightenment political theory, stressed the contract between the state and the individual and elevated state sovereignty over corporate self-interest, took Samuel's previously narrowly applied and utilitarian principle as justification for absolute loyalty to the state at the expense of Jewish law. They outdid each other in expressions of patriotism.

So it was that Jewish spokesmen downplayed the national or group characteristics of their faith and emphasised individual loyalty to the state. Jewish volunteers served in the Prussian army against Napoleonic France, and the women were said to be even more ardent patriots than the men, nursing wounded soldiers and organising war-effort charities. David Friedlander and other elders of the Berlin community encouraged young men to volunteer with the ringing words that it was 'a heavenly feeling to possess a fatherland! [...] Hand in hand with your fellow soldiers, you will complete the great task; they will not deny you the title of brother, for you will have earned it.'

In the enemy camp, when Napoleon convened an Assembly of Jewish Notables in 1806, its representatives answered a question about patriotism by declaring: 'In the eyes of every Israelite, without exception, submission to the prince is the first of duties. It is a principle generally acknowledged among them that, in everything related to civil or political interests, the law of the state is the *supreme* law.' In other words, a hallowed piece of Jewish legislation was being used against itself in order to justify obedience to the state in all matters save religious ritual. Within a few years, even the primacy of Jewish law in religious matters would be questioned, if it hampered progress towards speedier emancipation.

By the middle of the nineteenth century, Reform Judaism, a mere thirty years old, had become the majority movement among Germany's still-practising Jews. Its more radical antinomian elements were willing to transfer the Jewish Sabbath to Sunday and grant state control over marriage law for the sake of fuller integration into German society. It did indeed happen for a time that some Reform synagogues in Germany and the USA held Sunday services. Although the experiment did not catch on or survive long, it illustrated, in exaggerated form, the schisms that had been rumbling in organised Jewish life since the end of the Thirty Years War and glaringly brought to notice by the Enlightenment and the French Revolution. Henceforth, the rabbinic theology of a nation in exile on account of its sins could no longer be sustained in liberal European states working towards emancipation of their citizens.

9 REDEFINING THE JEW

After Napoleon's defeat at Waterloo, the aims of the victorious powers at the Congress of Vienna were to restore, as far as possible, the *status quo ante* and to reaffirm the principle of dynastic legitimacy. The Bourbons were reinstated in France. The German states, much reduced in number to thirty-nine, were assembled into a Germanic Confederation, on the dismembered remains of the Holy Roman Empire. German Jewry lobbied hard in Vienna to safeguard the rights it had acquired under Napoleon, but a mood of conservative reaction permeated Germany. A Romantic stress on blood, soil, Christian valour and Teutonic folk myth swept away the universalism of Enlightenment thought, suspiciously identified with the 'cosmopolitan' values of the French and the Jews. The Young German movement, with Goethe as its inspiration, advocated a specifically Germano-Christian national culture, arguing that Jews were Asiatic aliens who could not lay claim to such an identity without first converting.

In 1819 ugly riots against the Jews broke out in Bavaria and spread throughout Germany. Appalled Jewish witnesses felt that they had been transported back to the Dark Ages. Significantly, the rioting began in the university town of Würzburg, and the rallying cry of the mobs, *Hep! Hep!* (an acronym of the Latin *Hierosolyma est perdita*, 'Jerusalem is lost', originally attributed either to Roman soldiers at the siege of Jerusalem in 70 or to rampaging Crusaders in the Rhineland), suggested that the instigators were an educated cadre. Opposition to Jewish emancipation had been given intellectual respectability by an assortment of professors, pastors, writers and politicians who had rallied to the Young German movement and expressed themselves in inflammatory pamphlets with titles such as *On the Endangerment to the Prosperity and Character of the Germans by the Jews*, written by Jakob Friedrich Fries in 1816. This Heidelberg professor excused himself after the riots by explaining that his pamphlet had called only for the root and branch extermination of 'Judaism', not of Jews themselves. State governments discovered a convenient excuse in the riots for postponing or ignoring emancipatory legislation.

Progress towards full civil rights for Jews had been slowed but could not be halted. Conversion to Christianity increased but so did heightened Jewish activity to study and prune the ancestral faith, accentuate its similarities to Christianity and downplay any national element in Judaism that might preclude acceptance as citizens. An important factor in the growth of German Reform Judaism was its conscious adaptation to the contemporary Zeitgeist. New synagogues were built in the style of imposing public buildings, sermons and prayers were delivered in German and the liturgy was trimmed of all references to the rebuilding of the Temple or the Ingathering of the Exiles in Zion. Decorous congregants attended services at which an organ accompanied the mixed choir, dressing and comporting themselves like Sunday churchgoers.

The opponents of Reform, who called themselves Orthodox (i.e. conforming to traditional faith), denounced any modifications to practice and reiterated that the entire Torah, interpreted since ancient times by an unbroken chain of rabbinic tradition, was divinely revealed and therefore immutable. They too, though, defined the Jews as a religious, not a national, fellowship, united by the bond of obedience to divine law and therefore happily able to become full citizens in Germany, France and so forth.

A third movement, with links both to Reform and Orthodox yet bound to neither, made its appearance shortly after the *Hep! Hep!* riots. Shaken by the virulence of anti-Jewish feeling, a small group of exceptionally talented, university-educated young men met in Berlin to consider what had happened and what could be done to prevent a repetition. Their solution was to found a Society for the Culture and Scientific Study (*Wissenschaft*) of Judaism. Neither wedded uncritically to tradition, as were the Orthodox, nor willing to jettison it for modernity, as the Reformers appeared to be, the *Wissenschaft* movement looked for a middle way. Its principles were to study Jewish history systematically and non-dogmatically; to analyse the sacred texts of Judaism according to secular academic values; and to reconcile the Jewish heritage with German *Kultur* by undertaking a scientific study of the Jewish past based on the philological methods of the German universities and the vocabulary of Hegelian idealism, in order to best serve the overwhelming need of the present – how to rise to the challenge of emancipation.

Although the original Society did not last long, with two of its most gifted founders, Heinrich Heine and Eduard Gans, converting to Christianity, *Wissenschaft* methodology lasted until the advent of the Nazis, guiding and shaping Jewish scholarship of every denomination. Naturally, the exponents of *Wissenschaft* derived the message they desired from applying its methods. For the Reform movement, led by Abraham Geiger, a proper understanding of Jewish history legitimised religious adaptations and taught that the Jewish mission to be a light to the nations would attain its fullest expression when Judaism was recognised alongside Christianity as an essential component of the native German genius. For the Orthodox, led by Samson Raphael Hirsch, the lesson of Jewish history was that the Torah was a timeless, changeless pattern for the ideal life, and strict fidelity to tradition would not jeopardise the Jewish quest for emancipation because the essence of Judaism was not national but spiritual.

For all the apologetics of such people or the eloquent, libertarian essays of the baptised Ludwig Borne, it required the failed revolution of 1848 to stir shaken governments into reluctantly granting democratic concessions and civic equality for the adherents of all religions. When all of Germany except for Austria came under the German imperial constitution of 1871, the last restrictions on Jewish residence, marriage, choice of profession, acquisition of property and right to vote were abolished. Penning the Preface that year to the eleventh and final volume of his magisterial *History of the Jews*, Heinrich Graetz felt confident enough to write: 'Happier than any of my predecessors, I may conclude my history in the joyous feeling that in the civilised world the Jewish tribe [NB. not 'nation' or 'people'] has found at last not only justice and freedom but also recognition. Now at long last it has unlimited freedom to develop its talents, not as an act of [Christian] mercy but as a right acquired through thousandfold sufferings.'

But in indignantly rebutting, for the prize of civic equality, the canard that the Jews were 'a state within a state' the followers of *Wissenschaft* had rewritten the Jewish historical experience. The reality was that Jews had survived in the Diaspora, East and West, for eighteen hundred years precisely because they *had* maintained a discrete identity. As Theodor Herzl would shortly declare in his seminal 1896 pamphlet *Der Judenstaat* (*The Jewish State*), 'We are one people – our enemies have made us one whether we will it or not.'[1] Certainly in backward eastern Europe, where Russian rule extended over Lithuania, Poland, Galicia and Romania and the *Haskalah* movement emerged seventy years later than in Germany, the reality of Jewish nationhood, with five million Jews living a separate, cohesive existence, was accepted by *maskilim* and tsarist governments alike. The emancipated but deracinated Jewish assimilationists of western Europe, while by no means wishing to change places, would look with something like envy at their downtrodden but rooted eastern brethren.

It was axiomatic to stress Jewish powerlessness and portray mediaeval Jewish history as a saga of *Leiden und Lernen* (suffering and learning) in order to reassure German legislatures that they had nothing to fear from granting full citizenship to Jews. As a consequence, Jewish history was spiritualised in the telling. Isaac Marcus Jost, the forerunner of Graetz, opened his work on the Jews from the Maccabean period to modern times by asking, 'Can there be a history of slaves?'[2] He concluded that there could, if it was recognised that the 'true fatherland' of the Jews was God and religion. In a similar vein, Geiger argued that Judaism had survived precisely because it did not need a national framework; its rabbis and teachers of the Second Temple period had been universal ethical monotheists – that is, the very model of nineteenth-century Reform Jews.

Graetz was arguably the greatest of all the *Wissenschaft* practitioners whose thesis was that the harmony of religion and politics is exemplified in ideal form by the history of Judaism, a unique politico-religious organism 'whose soul is the Torah and whose body is the Holy Land'. He affirmed that the Jews became a spiritual people once they lost their state, giving up political power for intellectual and religious attainments. He dismissed Reform's overhaul of belief and pruning of ritual as bartering the past for emancipation, described Samuel Holdheim, a radical Reform rabbi, as the greatest enemy of Judaism since Paul of Tarsus and vowed to fight against what he called 'the Christianisation of Judaism' with all the weapons at his command. But, in the Preface to the fifth volume of his *magnum opus,* he wrote that '[h]istory still has not produced another case of a nation which has laid aside its weapons of war to devote itself entirely to the peaceful pursuits of study and poetry, which has freed itself of self-interest and let its thoughts soar to fathom its own nature'.

A new stereotype of the Jew was being constructed by these apologists for gentile acceptance. Instead of the law-bound Old Testament nomad, the New Testament Christ-killer, the mediaeval moneylender, the slippery cosmopolitan of popular imagination, a victimised, politically impotent but spiritually elevated individual was waiting to take his place gratefully in modern society.

The Bible is replete with bloodthirsty events. The first Jewish Commonwealth survived by the sword and perished by the sword. The Maccabees briefly restored Judean sovereignty by warfare. An orgy of political assassinations and hopeless struggle against the military might of Rome preceded the destruction of the Second Temple. There were further large-scale insurrections against Rome in Alexandria and under Bar Kochba. Chasdai ibn Shaprut, Samuel ha-Nagid, Don Isaac Abravenal and Joseph Nasi, Duke of Naxos, were among several examples of Diaspora Jews rising to high military or diplomatic position. Throughout the Middle Ages, Jewish communities defended themselves where they could or took up arms in defence of their host cities. In sixteenth-century Venice, rabbinic enactments permitted young Jewish bloods to wear their swords on the Sabbath. Court Jews had grown wealthy by learning about cavalry horses, muskets, cannon and ammunition. During the Napoleonic Wars, thirteen hundred Prussian Jews had served in the army and seventy-one had been awarded the Iron Cross for bravery.

Notwithstanding such historical evidence to the contrary, *Wissenschaft* scholars discovered that Rabbinic Judaism's most prized ideal was peace (justice would have been a more plausible candidate) and that, since the exile from their ancient homeland, Jews had transformed themselves into a pacifist, religiously studious and subservient people much put upon by bigoted and heartless Christianity (the world of Islam and its Jews was virtually a closed book to European Jewry), indifferent to nationalism (despite several false Messiahs, of whom Shabbetai Tzevi was the most notorious, having emerged to lead the Jews back to their land) and desirous only of acceptance by their host countries.

Needless to say, it was an oversimplified picture. By concentrating on Jewish suffering throughout the ages – what nowadays we would call 'a culture of victimhood' – this nineteenth-century stereotype was embraced both by its Jewish advocates and philo-Semites such as George Eliot. *Daniel*

Deronda is a novel of overt special pleading that the Jews, who took precedence over all nations in the ranks of suffering (an idea Eliot lifted from her reading of the *Wissenschaft* scholar Leopold Zunz), should be encouraged to fulfil their mission of rebuilding a national homeland in Palestine. That is the goal to which the noble, eponymous hero devotes his life.

This sedulously cultivated but dangerously quiescent image of the Jewish victim helplessly buffeted by fate could be said to have reached its self-fulfilling apogee in the metaphor of the six million passively going into the Nazi death camps 'like sheep to the slaughter'. But already, well before the Second World War, its prevalence had prompted the early Zionists scornfully to reject it and create instead their model of the 'new', upright and consciously different Jew.

10 ZIONISTS, SOCIALISTS, OLD JEWS, 'NEW' HEBREWS

As the nineteenth century drew to its close, European Jewry was in a state of flux and confusion. On the one hand, emancipation and assimilation had brought about a remarkable improvement in the status and *embourgeoisement* of Jews living in Germany, France, the Austro-Hungarian Empire and other liberal states; on the other hand, the avidity with which they seized the opportunities offered in education, commerce and the professions provoked a counter-reaction from all those elements in society that felt most threatened by their success. A new phenomenon, anti-Semitism (the term was coined in 1873 by William Marr, a gutter journalist and baptised son of a Jewish actor), based on economic fear and pseudo-scientific anthropological findings that 'proved' the superiority of Aryan peoples over Asiatic ones, had replaced the mediaeval Judeophobia encouraged by Church teachings. Political parties, jealous business competitors and landed gentry pained by the 'new money-aristocracy' could all make use of the catchphrase of Heinrich von Treitschke, a respected Prussian historian, that 'the Jews are our misfortune!' Adolf Stöcker, court chaplain to the kaiser, was elected to the Reichstag in 1881 on a rabidly anti-Semitic platform. Karl Lueger was voted in as mayor of Vienna in 1895 by playing on the same fears of the Catholic working classes, although, with two million Jews spread throughout his territories and to his credit, 'Papa' Franz-Joseph refused to sanction his election. In France, the Dreyfus Affair was splitting families and threatening the fabric of society.

In eastern Europe, the five million Jews under Russian rule faced a different threat. There, the practical steps towards liberalising their condition initiated during the reign of Tsar Alexander II were abruptly reversed after his assassination in 1881. A wave of pogroms erupted against Jewish communities, probably with government connivance, since the authorities only moved belatedly to quell the rioters, because they suspected Jewish involvement in anarchist and socialist groups.

It was around this time that two new ideologies joined the *Haskalah*, religious reform and assimilation as Jewish responses to emancipation. One was Zionism and the other Socialism. After the pogroms of 1881, numerous small societies had sprung up in the towns and villages of Russia's so-called 'Pale of Settlement' (the twenty-five provinces in which Jews were officially permitted to reside), calling for a Jewish revival in Palestine. The first pioneers, a group of Kharkov university students, decided upon immediate emigration to set up a farming cooperative on socialist principles. Thirteen men and one woman eventually arrived in Jaffa at the beginning of July 1882. Two years later, these proliferating *Chibbat Zion* (Love of Zion) societies convened their first conference in Upper Silesia, just across the border from Russian Poland.

Their president, an Odessa physician called Judah Leib Pinsker, had achieved notoriety with an anonymously published pamphlet entitled *Auto-Emancipation: A Warning to His People by a Russian Jew*. In it, Pinsker diagnosed anti-Semitism as a hereditary, incurable pathology, castigated his fellow Jews for bartering their Jewish heritage for the delusion of civil rights and insisted that the only remedy was a collective, national one, because 'a people without a territory is like a man without a shadow; something unnatural, spectral'.[1]

Pinsker had written his short pamphlet in German for two reasons. First, he was convinced that only western Jewry had the capacity and means to rescue the eastern European masses and it was their support he wanted to enlist; and, second, more prosaically, had he written his essay in Russian, it would not have found its way past the censor.

Russian Socialism was the counter-attraction to Russian Zionism. The Marxist dialectic appealed especially to *Haskalah*-educated, Russified Jews. The authorities were justified in suspecting Jewish involvement in all the radical movements that threatened the tsar's autocratic regime. Throughout the cities of the Pale, activists were organising embryonic trade unions and agitating for better working conditions. Zionists dismissed the aim of full Jewish equality within an egalitarian Russia as a pious hope; only a Jewish homeland would eradicate the problem of anti-Semitism. For their part, Jewish socialists condemned Zionism as a deluded form of 'romantic bourgeois nationalism'. Their chief pre-occupation was in trying to reconcile the contradiction between maintaining a specific Jewish identity and espousing international Socialism, given that, in an ideal Marxist state, Jewish separatism would disappear once the capitalist economic structure which promoted it had been overthrown.

It took Theodor Herzl, extraordinary *poseur*, restless obsessive, publicity manipulator of genius and founder of the Zionist movement, to bring together the various Zionist factions of eastern and western Europe at his first Zionist Congress in Basle in 1897. Significantly, just five and a half weeks later, a group of Jewish workers met in Vilna to form the General Union of Jewish Workers in Lithuania, Poland and Russia (the *Bund*), with the aims of raising the level of Jewish political consciousness, creating self-defence groups and allying to the Russian Labour movement on the basis of partnership rather than assimilation.

The *Bund* became far more popular than Zionism for Russian Jewry, even though the revolutionary socialist Leon Trotsky derided its leaders as 'Zionists who are afraid to become seasick' because of their forlorn advocacy of an autonomous Jewish territory within a Russian republic. Many thousands joined the *Bund*, whereas never more than two per cent of the Jewish population immigrated to Palestine between 1882 and 1903. But the majority of Russian Jews had no time for either Zionism or the *Bund*. After the pogroms of 1881, those who could fled from eastern Europe to more hospitable lands. In all, nearly three million Jews migrated from the Russian Empire between 1881 and the start of the First World War: over two million to the USA, 200,000 to Great Britain, 40,000 to South Africa, 100,000 to Canada and approximately 300,000 elsewhere in Europe. In contrast, only 45–50,000 reached Palestine during the same period, and well over half of those left, usually for America.

The ones who stayed, known collectively as the First *Aliyah* (Ascent) and the Second *Aliyah*, were the pioneers of Labour Zionism. They were joined between 1919 and 1923 by some 35,000 immigrants of the Third *Aliyah*, most of whom had lived through the Russian Revolution and were influenced by Marxism and radical Socialism in all its picayune splinter groups. This was the politically aware, socialist-imbued generation that gave the Jewish settlement in Palestine its distinctive, collectivist ethos. It was they who wished to make explicit the difference between the Diaspora Jew and the 'new' Jew. The metamorphosis in the social condition of Jewry brought about by settling the land would be accompanied by a spiritual and physical transformation. Writers of the First *Aliyah* era (1882–1903) boasted about the changed appearance of the youth living in Palestine – strong, muscled from work in the fields, self-confident – compared to their pale, soft Diaspora counterparts.[2]

In the Diaspora too, as Jews gained admittance into gentile society, emphasis was placed on manly, physical activities. For those who could not aspire to cavalry regiments or duelling fraternities, sports clubs with names redolent of a heroic Jewish past, such as the Young Maccabees or Bar Kochba, opened in Germany, the Austro-Hungarian Empire and Russia, encouraging young Jews to play athletic games. Max Nordau, one of Herzl's most ardent followers and a bombastic social analyst, despaired of degenerate Diaspora life and called for 'Judaism with muscles'. Micah Berdichevsky, a Talmudic prodigy from a notable Russian rabbinic family, who had been thrown out by his scandalised father-in-law for secretly studying forbidden Enlightenment literature, left to enrol at the University of Breslau, where he became a Jewish disciple of Nietzsche. He adapted the concept of the Superman to a Jewish context; the timid and persecuted Jew would be remoulded as an *Übermensch*. The Jews had reached a stage of almost total decay. As a consequence, 'some leave the House of Israel to venture among foreign peoples, devoting to them the service of their hearts and offering their strength to strangers; while, at the other extreme, the pious sit in their gloomy caverns ...'. The solution was to cease following an abstract and petrified Judaism and opt instead for a life-enhancing nationalism. A fateful choice faced the people: 'We are the last Jews – or we are the first of a new nation.'[3]

Jewish Marxists, nationalists, territorialists, utopian socialists, Tolstoyan agrarians and Nietzschean romantics all had their say on how to identify and solve the Jewish problem. Common to all was a sense that a bright, new and, most of all, young world awaited. The cult of youth was a by-product of the European nationalism that flourished in the latter half of the nineteenth and the beginning of the twentieth centuries. The old order was crumbling, as entrenched societies were forced to accommodate to the pace of techno-industrial progress, the spread of capitalism, enhanced communications and large movements of people who sought economic betterment. Shortly, the Communist Revolution would destroy for ever the familiar European world of monarchy, hierarchy and deference.

This rebellion against the timidity of their elders, who had, cap in hand, sought acceptance from anti-Semitic ruling cliques, was symbolised in Jewry by Zionism, the 'young' nationalist movement. With his acute sensitivity to the mood of the moment, Herzl had exhorted in 1901: 'Join together, young men. We need you. You must be strong and upstanding. We need your strength and your knowledge. Until now, "Jewish boys" was an insult. Turn that around. Make it into a name of honour.'

Such attempts to overturn the traditional image of the Jew as a pallid, physically insignificant student poring over pages of the Talmud were only partially successful, and even then only in countries such as Germany, where the bourgeoisie had been acculturating for several generations. In eastern Europe, Jewish life in the towns and small villages still conformed to the unflattering stereotype of anti-Semites and liberated Zionists alike. In their robust rejection of their Diaspora past, the early settlers in Palestine expressed themselves in language that smacked of self-hatred, as if to confirm the acuity of Arthur Koestler's admission that he became a communist out of hatred for the poor and a Zionist out of hatred for the 'Yid'. An unparalleled historical example of a small, homeless and dispersed people managing to survive for two millennia by means of resilience, adaptability and religious faith wherever fate happened to land them was being dismissed as shameful, embarrassing and unworthy. Geographical distancing was symptomatic of a deeper cultural split that henceforth would offer either Zionist or Diaspora perceptions of what it meant to be a Jew. A demarcation line was being drawn between old Jew and 'new Hebrew'. Nowadays, that distinction is sharper than ever before.

11 ZIONISM FOR THE FEW, INTEGRATION FOR THE MANY

At the ceremonial Passover meal celebrated by Jews, the story of the Exodus from Egypt is read from the *Haggadah*, a text that dates from the ninth century CE, some three thousand different versions of which have been compiled since the invention of printing. Common to all is a homily concerning the Four Sons, one wise, one wicked (*rasha*), one simple and one too young to ask questions. In mediaeval versions of the *Haggadah*, many of them elaborately illustrated and valuable works of art, the wicked son is frequently depicted as a soldier. Above the armed and swaggering *rasha* of the 1526 Prague *Haggadah* is a caption in Hebrew that reads: 'Woe to the wicked son and woe to his neighbour.'

From illustrations such as these, sanctimonious commentators and didactic rabbis liked to draw the moral that, because of their long history of persecution and martyrdom at the hands of gentile soldiery, Jews had an in-built aversion to warfare – conveniently overlooking the fact that the wicked soldier son in the illustration is meant to be a *Jew*! There is no reason to suppose that the Jewish genetic inheritance is more pacific than that of other peoples. Apart from the examples already given of mediaeval Jewish participation in urban defence or self-defence where they were permitted to bear arms, it is worth noting that a Polish folk hero was the Jew Berek Joselowicz, who raised a volunteer battalion of Jewish cavalry during the 1794 rebellion against Russia. After Napoleon created the Duchy of Warsaw, Joselowicz was appointed a commander, and fell while leading a charge against the Austrians. Conscription, for terms of up to twenty-five years, was imposed upon young Jews during the reign of Tsar Nicholas I.

Nevertheless, it accorded with the image of the Jew favoured by both *bien pensant* Enlightenment thinkers and Jews themselves who were pushing for emancipation to stress the non-aggressive Jewish qualities – studiousness, modesty, hard work and loyalty to the state. Intellectuals of the calibre of Moses Mendelssohn and his circle were a more attractive example of Jewish potential to set before dubious legislatures than the typical peddler or the à la mode children of parvenu merchants. This burnished image of nobly borne suffering provided downtrodden Jews, especially in Russian-ruled territories, with a palliative for their lowly condition. God's Chosen People might be enduring a long, hard exile, but, unlike the neighbouring peasants, they did not drink to excess or fight. The prayer hall and the house of study were their refuge. Among some *Chasidic* circles, this sense of Jewish cultural difference became the obverse of anti-Semitic stereotyping; the Jewish soul was inherently superior, more refined and less warlike than that of the goyim.

Throughout the villages and hamlets of the Pale of Settlement, the parental dream for a son was that he grew up to be a Talmudic scholar or, if they lived in a city and were dangerously free-thinking, that he should be *Haskalah*-educated at least. The prayer for a daughter was that she contracted a wealthy marriage. It was understood, in pariah imitation of a Chekhov play, that the pale, bony *yeshivah* student unsuited for manual work would be supported by the community while the women got on with providing for the family. The musical *Fiddler on the Roof* is a saccharine version of *shtetl* aspiration, minus the dirt, superstition and backwardness, the relentless *sameness* of daily existence.

It was precisely this image of the Jew that the early Zionists wished to overturn. A key word in the vocabulary of First and Second *Aliyah* pioneers was 'Hebrew', rather than 'Jew'. With its biblical antecedents and connection to the land, the term 'Hebrew' was consciously used to distinguish the settler in Palestine from the Jew in the Diaspora. A Hebrew was different, 'gentile' in appearance and outlook. Tilling the soil, raising cattle, living outdoors in a sunny climate and eating a healthy diet, the native-born Hebrew was the mental and physical antithesis of his indoor-living, east European and bookish counterpart. As an early pioneer song put it, the Jews would 'rebuild themselves in building the land'. Not only would Zionism take the Jew out of the ghetto, the ghetto, with all its materialistic concerns and limited horizons, would be taken out of the Jew. The apostle of this creed was A. D. Gordon, a mystical pantheist of the Tolstoyan school and eccentric, middle-aged curiosity among the ardent, young pioneers. He exalted physical labour and communion with Nature in ecstatic paeans to the redemptive qualities of work (which in Hebrew is the same word as 'religious service').

The new breed of Jew had to undertake military duties. It was a shock to the socialist-inspired ideals of the early settlers on their collective farms, anxious to do their own menial tasks and not exploit the Arab peasantry, to discover that the natives reacted resentfully and violently to their coming. In order to protect lives, crops and property, a paramilitary organisation, *Ha-Shomer* (The Guard), was established. Its members soon acquired cult status as independent warriors patrolling the hills of Galilee on their horses, rifle in hand and wearing traditional Arab headdress.

In other ways, too, the Palestinian pioneers set out to destroy anything associated with the humiliations of a Diaspora past. The nucleus of the Third *Aliyah* (1919–1923), in particular, was radically left-wing, provocatively experimental and scornful of bourgeois *mores* as it looked to establish its blueprint of the ideal society. Even in Herzl's time, twenty years before, it had been a wry joke that the definition of a Zionist was a Jew who solicited money from a second Jew to send a third Jew to Palestine. The young men and women of the Third *Aliyah*, many of them veterans of the Bolshevik Revolution, were dismissive of the generation that had helped pay their fare.

The social group that had predominated in the Zionist Organisation since its founding by Herzl was overwhelmingly middle-class, Eurocentric, politically liberal, humanist in outlook and accustomed to pursuing its aims through the well-worn Diaspora channels of patronage, influence and quiet diplomacy. The firebrands of the Third *Aliyah* wanted to eradicate precisely this ingratiating way of getting things done. At issue was a fathers-and-sons conflict between the Diaspora experience of the 'old' Jew and the impatient expectation of the 'new' Hebrew.

Many of these new Hebrews belonged to the *Ha-shomer Ha-tza'ir* (The Young Watchman) youth group founded in Galicia during the First World War. They were middle-class, well-educated social revolutionaries, rejecting the conventional family ties and hypocritical compromises of their elders back in the Diaspora. Their inspiration came from Marxist theory, the psychoanalytical concepts of Freud, the romantic ideas of the Free German Youth movement and the windy philosophy of Martin Buber in his patriotic *Blut und Boden* (Blood and Soil) phase. It is surprising to learn that the irenic religious philosopher of famous old age could, in an earlier incarnation, address to Zionist youth such neo-Romantic, pseudo-Marxist sentiments as 'a truly Jewish commonwealth can be none other than one in which the precepts of Moses with regard to the equalisation of property, the appeals of the Prophets for social justice, are translated into reality ... Upon you, upon the youth, will it depend ...'

The first kibbutz, Bet Alfa, founded by these young pioneers in 1922, was far more daring than any of the farming cooperatives set up by the previous generation. Children slept in a children's house, not with their parents. All meals were eaten together; solitary dining was deemed to be asocial and a residue of bourgeois upbringing. Religion, of course, was dismissed as an irrational neurosis. Dance, collective decision-making, communal eating and regular group confessionals replaced the rituals and ceremonies of Diaspora Judaism as the new sacred rites. There was an unconscious irony in this. The young kibbutzniks were unaware that they were replicating in a secular guise the east European village life they had been so keen to escape. As in the Pale of Settlement, where communal life was regulated by rabbinic ordinance, a kibbutz community depended upon supportive neighbours, an insular group identity and conformity to corporate institutions and norms. Indeed, in their intense personal relationships and ideological fervour, the early communes most closely resembled a *Chasidic* sect, a resemblance which some pioneers recognised. '*Chasidism* is the spring from which we drew our songs and nourished our souls in those first days,' remembered a kibbutz veteran forty years on.[1] The very word 'kibbutz' originated with the Bratislaver *Chasidim* from the Ukraine, who so labelled their gatherings to pray at the grave of their founder on the Jewish New Year festival.

It scandalised Orthodox Jews and Arab *fellahin* alike that men and women worked the fields in the same-sex uniform of shorts and shirt/blouse, as well as the fact that the family unit apparently had been discarded for free love. But there was an endearing puritanism underlying this avowal of sexual liberation. Couples wanting to consummate their attraction for each other would inform the kibbutz secretariat that they wished to 'become one family', as their coy euphemism for moving into a joint room. Any children who resulted were fed a diet of classical music and art once they became adolescents, to sublimate their libidinous urges into productive channels.

Seemingly, there was little in common between the conservative, religiously based value system of Diaspora Jews and the overwhelmingly socialist and secular innovations of Zionist pioneers. How could they possibly work together? Until the middle of the twentieth century, colonising in Palestine was of little concern to most of the world's sixteen million Jews. According to the first British Mandate census of 1922, there were 84,000 Jews in the *Yishuv* (Settlement, the term used to describe the Jewish community of Palestine prior to statehood). The Arab riots of 1920 and 1921, and the still more violent ones of 1929, evoked sympathy and concern from the Jews of Europe and America, but, insofar as they held an opinion about Zionism, the normative Orthodox view was expressed by the German rabbi who declared: 'The attempt of Zionism to lead Israel, nation and land, into the "normalcy" of the other nations has no future. It is only God's kingly will, God's revealed Torah, that can shelter Israel, the people and the land.' As for American Reform Judaism, the Pittsburgh Platform of 1885 echoed earlier statements of German Reform by rejecting prayers for a return to Zion in favour of Israel's great Messianic hope for the establishment of truth, justice and peace among all men. By the time of the Columbus Platform fifty-two years later, the influence on its content of leading Zionist sympathisers such as Rabbis Stephen Wise and Abba Hillel Silver, allied to the alarming evidence of Nazi treatment of Germany's Jews, produced a qualified endorsement to aid in building up the Jewish homeland so that it might become 'a centre of Jewish culture and spiritual life'. Achad Ha-Am's ideal of cultural Zionism was acceptable, but the by-now-undisguised aim of the Zionist leadership to achieve statehood, despite Arab opposition, was a cause for concern.

Perhaps it was Freud who most percipiently expressed the ambivalent response to Zionism of the majority of acculturated Western Jews, of whatever religious affiliation or none. In an address to the Viennese branch of the *B'nei Brith* organisation on his seventieth birthday in 1926, he stated: 'Whenever I felt an inclination to national enthusiasm, I strove to suppress it as being harmful and wrong, alarmed by the warning examples of the peoples among whom we Jews had lived.'[2] Four years later, he declined the request sent to prominent European Jews by the Jewish Agency to criticise the British government's restriction on Jewish immigration to Palestine and access to pray at the Western Wall after the Arab riots, replying: 'Whoever wants to influence the masses must give them something rousing and inflammatory and my sober judgement of Zionism does not permit this.' He expressed his sympathy with the achievements of Zionism – the Hebrew University in Jerusalem, the thriving agricultural settlements – but would not put his name to inflamed national identification. 'I can claim no sympathy at all for the misdirected piety which transforms a piece of a Herodian wall into a national relic, thus offending the feelings of the natives.' He wanted no part of national identity raised to fever pitch. 'It would have seemed more sensible to me to establish a Jewish homeland on a less historically burdened land... But I know that such a rational viewpoint would never have gained the enthusiasm of the masses and the financial support of the wealthy.'[3] Freud's concern about political Zionism arose from his distrust of the group mind fanning the flame of nationalist passions.

The Zionist minority, with its goal of statehood, was beginning to exert disproportionate pressure on collective Jewry. Even so, it would take the Second World War and the horrifying evidence of Nazism's attempt to exterminate European Jewry to persuade almost all Jews, apart from fringe groups of the ultra-religious right or the far left of Socialism, that now they were indeed Zionists. But we should not get ahead of our story.

12 THE GOLDEN AGE OF GERMAN JEWRY

Kurt Blumenfeld, the son of a district judge in East Prussia, was elected president of the German Zionist Federation in 1909 at the tender age of twenty-five. He advised Zionist youth to study Nietzsche in order to become 'stronger' Jews. At the annual conference of 1912, he successfully persuaded delegates to affirm the duty of all Zionists, especially those of independent means, to 'include emigration to Palestine in their life programme'.

Blumenfeld himself did not practise what he preached until 1933, after Hitler came to power. Until his death thirty years later in what was now the State of Israel, his cultural idol was Goethe. The ideals of *Bildung* and Kantian universalism were more deeply rooted in his soul than the imperatives of pioneering.

At the same time, by way of contrast, the Zionist young in Palestine were being taught an ethnocentric and ideologically committed version of history that emphasised the Jewish people's moral and intellectual contributions to humanity and insisted repetitively on Jewish martyrology through the ages and, as a logical corollary, on the inevitable necessity of the Zionist solution to the perennial Jewish problem.

More than any other sphere, education highlighted the diverging world-views of *Yishuv* and Diaspora Jews. The first manual of *Ha-Shomer Ha-tza'ir*, the Zionist youth movement, published in Warsaw in 1917, stated: 'Our intention is to educate a young Hebrew of solid muscles, strong will, healthy and normal thought without convolutions or sophistry, disciplined, a Jew with all his heart.' Rejection of the Diaspora involved not only forsaking the impossible dream of assimilation into gentile society but also abandoning the traditional Jewish way of life with its emphasis on the study of sacred texts. The immigrants of the Second (1904–1914) and Third (1919–1923) *Aliyah* were scornful of the east European houses of study in which they themselves had been taught. Ideologues such as Micah Berdichevsky fiercely denounced the degenerate religiosity that was snuffing out the *élan vital* of Jewish nationhood. Rabbinic teachings about forbearance in the face of suffering had encouraged further calamities. Now was the time for Jews to embrace outdoor life instead of the synagogue and change their people's destiny through manual labour rather than study.

One of the most strident debates among the early Zionists was about which language to use in the new country. Herzl, in his pamphlet *The Jewish State* and his utopian romance *Altneuland*, appears to assume that German will be the lingua franca, with Yiddish for the lower classes and Hebrew, like the Latin Mass, reserved for liturgical purposes. The pioneers wanted no truck with Yiddish, the language of their degradation, refused to countenance German or English as betokening cultural imperialism and barely considered Arabic, the language of culturally backward peoples in whose midst they intended to settle. So Hebrew it would be, but shorn of its high literary style in biblical and rabbinic writings, turned into a practical, secular language and taken to the street. Eliezer Ben-Yehudah (formerly Perelmann) and other philologists on the Hebrew Language Council invented scores of neologisms to meet the exigencies of modern civilisation, with its telephones, tractors, aeroplanes and railways.

The Bible still served as a crucial educational tool but not as the repository of Jewish faith. It was studied in schools from a secular, nationalist perspective, linking the Jewish people's mythological past to its pioneering present. On occasion, this required a contorted re-evaluation of the facts, as in the case of the prophet Jeremiah and the manner in which an educator recommended that his opposition to holding out in Jerusalem against the Babylonians should be presented. By most standards, Jeremiah would be deemed a fifth columnist, spreading doom and gloom among the besieged defenders. When the exiles were carried off to Babylon, he wrote his famous letter to the captives, urging them to pray for the welfare of their new rulers and to resume normal life. For A. Urinovsky, 'the rational, practical prophet' had an ingenious deeper purpose in mind. Worthy of special emphasis was 'his uncompromising, tragic struggle for his people's existence in their land. He preferred the shame of surrender and temporary enslavement to utter political destruction with honour, which leads to exile, to the uprooting of the tree from the place it sprouted and grew...'[1] Evidently Jeremiah, among his other talents, had been blessed with the gift of foresight and therefore knew that Cyrus would defeat the Babylonians sixty years later and permit the exiles to return.

Biblical heroes such as Samson, Gideon and King David were exalted, implicit role models for the modern farmer-warriors defending their kibbutzim from Arab raiders. Post-biblical figures such as Judah the Maccabee, Eleazar ben-Yair, the doomed commander of Masada, and Bar Kochba, the leader of the last, failed insurrection against Rome, were given more prominence in the curriculum for their glorious martial failures than were religious giants such as Rashi, Maimonides, Ibn Ezra and Moses Mendelssohn for their sedentary intellectual achievements.

Hebrew civilisation was made the epicentre of all civilisations, the yardstick by which others were evaluated. World history was taught through the narrow prism of how it had impinged upon the Jews, as in the joke about the Jewish boy who is given a homework assignment about the elephant and hands in an essay entitled 'The Elephant and the Jewish Problem'.

Arthur Koestler served as a foreign correspondent in Palestine in the 1920s and his beady eye and mordant wit at the expense of the humourless ideological rectitude of the pioneers made him a favourite hate figure. He paid a visit to the Herzliya Gymnasium, the jewel in the *Yishuv*'s pedagogical crown, and afterwards noted in his diary the egocentric method of teaching history, with the Bible as the main source for studying antiquity and Israel as the hub of the ancient world. The confused events of the Dark and Middle Ages were reduced to a series of barbarian anticlockwise migrations around the Mediterranean, with the Jews moving clockwise. It all reminded him of his first school in Budapest. The Hungarians, a small nation perched precariously between the Slavonic and Germanic worlds, 'were inclined towards this kind of mystical ultra-chauvinism'.[2]

The joint authors of *The History of Our People*, a standard textbook of the time, were explicit in stating that ethnocentrism was indeed the purpose of their endeavour. 'We have integrated the history of the nations into the history of our nation in a restricted and concentrated way, so as not to distract the student ... We have made room for the history of different nations at those junctures in which they came into contact with our nation.'[3]

It is a fact that all societies in the throes of revolutionary change are self-absorbed and regard events in the outside world as incidental to their own momentous undertaking. In Palestine during the early years of the twentieth century, this isolation was accentuated by geographical distance. With aviation in its infancy, travel from Europe to the Holy Land usually required either a leisurely sea voyage or a hazardous overland journey. The communal farms of the *Yishuv* were self-contained entities, scattered around the landscape. Tel Aviv, nowadays a bustling metropolis, had been founded as a small village in 1909 on the sand dunes outside Jaffa. Jerusalem, where Jews had outnumbered other nationalities since the mid-nineteenth century, was a languishing backwater, mainly inhabited by the pious Orthodox. The German Reform rabbi who decried Zionism as 'Palestinian provincialism' could be excused his dismissive judgement when it really did seem, for the first three decades of the twentieth century, that German Jewry had entered its golden age.

For one thing, German Jewry was extremely prosperous. Of the two hundred wealthiest Prussian families, forty were Jewish. In Berlin, the Jews numbered about sixty thousand, or five per cent of the total population, but paid more than thirty per cent of the municipal taxes. Twenty per cent of high school students were Jewish. An express bus, nicknamed the 'Roaring Moses', carried bankers and brokers every morning from their palatial villas in the Grunewald forest to Berlin's newly built stock exchange. In Frankfurt, the tax paid by Jews was on average four times higher than that of Protestants and eight times that of Catholics.

An embarrassing blot on this prosperity, and one exploited by anti-Semites, was the flood of impoverished refugees who streamed across Germany's eastern border after the 1881 pogroms. By the turn of the century, up to fifteen per cent of the Jewish population was foreign-born. Between 1882 and 1914, well over a million Jews used Germany as a transit stage on their way to the USA, South America and Great Britain. Their shabby, impoverished presence alienated assimilated co-religionists, whose charitable organisations moved the newcomers on as quickly as possible. Gustav Mahler bewailed being related to them and Walter Rathenau, a future German foreign minister, fulminated against the 'Asiatic horde' flooding in. The *Centralverein*, the representative body of German Jewry founded in 1893, was careful to distinguish its patriotic credentials from those of Jewish transients: 'We are not German Jews. We are German citizens of the Jewish faith.'

By then, however, the ugly spurt of anti-Semitism occasioned by a stock market collapse in the wake of the Franco-Prussian war and fanned by the rabble-rousing sermons of Adolf Stöcker, the court chaplain, and the fastidious jeremiads of Heinrich von Treitschke, Prussia's leading historian, had largely subsided. Stöcker lost his post and Treitschke was denounced by Theodor Mommsen, a fellow historian at the University of Berlin, and seventy-five professorial colleagues who signed a petition deploring racism. If the high water mark of political anti-Semitism appeared to be in 1893, when various anti-Semitic parties had sixteen deputies between them elected to the Reichstag, a more significant straw in the wind had been in the election nine years previously, when Paul Singer, a Jewish candidate, comprehensively defeated a prominent anti-Semite. In the general election results of 1912, anti-Semitic splinter parties virtually disappeared. The Social Democratic Party, campaigning against anti-Semitic 'Junkers, priests, knights and Christian saints', won thirty-five per cent of the popular vote. The number of Jewish deputies rose from eight to nineteen, twelve of whom were Social Democrats.

German Jewry flourished in this auspicious climate. Among Germans and their uneasy rivals alike, there was a growing feeling that unification, material and military strength and intellectual vigour in culture and the sciences would make it Germany's turn to dominate Europe in the new century. German Jews were prominent in spearheading the advance. They were avid patrons of the arts, often ridiculed for their parvenu pretensions; certainly, it was ironic that Jews were among the most fervent admirers of Wagner's music, financing the construction of that rabid anti-Semite's concert hall in Bayreuth. Jewish collectors and benefactors helped to turn Berlin into a major art metropolis. There were thirty-one major donors to the National Gallery prior to the First World War, twenty-eight of them Jewish. German Jews were equally keen supporters of the theatre and literary talent. They were so active as publishers, playwrights, theatre directors, artists, writers, musicians and critics that in 1912 a young Jewish journalist incautiously claimed that Jews now controlled German culture. Thomas Mann felt it necessary to refute rumours that he, too, was a Jew (although his wife Katia was of Jewish descent).

Most remarkable of all was the Jewish contribution in the sciences. German universities led the field in scientific research. Spectacular advances in the realms of medicine, chemistry, biology, mathematics and physics culminated in Einstein's theory of relativity. But he was merely the best-known of thirty-nine leading German Jewish scientists, ten of whom won Nobel Prizes. One of them, Paul Ehrlich, directed an eponymous institute that rivalled in prestige the Pasteur in

Paris or the Rockefeller in New York. At the recently founded Kaiser Wilhelm Institute in Berlin, a leading centre of advanced research, the four main departments were led by Jews and significantly funded by Jewish philanthropists.

In banking, commerce and industry, the most significant institutions were founded or controlled by Jews. Gerson von Bleichröder, Bismarck's private banker, whose palatial residence in Berlin had stunned Disraeli, among others, with its florid opulence, had been reckoned the richest man in Germany; but even his wealth paled beside the fortunes amassed by the Jewish directors of the new corporate and state banks, among them the Reichsbank and the Deutsche Bank, that provided industry with the capital for expansion. (It is a poignant sidelight on the subsequent fate of German Jewry that many of the next generation of the Bleichröder family converted to Christianity or chose alternative careers. Some even became members of the Nazi Party and friends of Hitler's inner circle, to no avail. One of the few who survived the Holocaust was a great-nephew, Rudolf, who had been sent to London as a banker and received a prescient cable on Hitler's appointment as chancellor in 1933 telling him on no account to return to Germany. The author conducted his funeral in 2000.)

The German aircraft industry and first department store chains were established by Jews. Albert Ballin, head of the Hamburg-America Line, was one of the world's greatest shipping magnates. Walter Rathenau's father, Emil, was known as the 'Bismarck of the German electric industry' for introducing electric light and trams to most German cities under the banner of his AEG company.

The financial power and industrial importance of such individuals brought them into personal acquaintance with the kaiser, who retained the prejudices of his Junker class but was fascinated by self-made men. They were known disparagingly as *Kaiserjuden* (the kaiser's Jews), a term coined by the Russian Zionist leader Chaim Weizmann, who was contemptuous of them for being 'more German than the Germans ... super-patriotic, eagerly anticipating the wishes and plans of the masters of Germany'.

It is hardly surprising that such successful entrepreneurs, eminent scientists, physicians and academics, as well as the hundreds of thousands of aspiring petty tradesmen and anonymous artisans who hoped that if not they, at least their children, would emulate them and among whom it was joked that *Doktor* was a Jewish first name, had little enthusiasm for the picayune Zionist enterprise in faraway Palestine. Complacent about ever-greater acceptance, intermarriage among German Jews reached thirty per cent by 1915 and baptism over twenty per cent, despite the dire prediction of a Zionist doctor that between them intermarriage and a declining birth rate would lead to the disappearance of German Jewry by 1950.

The publication of Theodor Herzl's *Der Judenstaat* (*The Jewish State*) in 1896 had been greeted by European Jewry with isolated enthusiasm, widespread indifference and sharp rejection, nowhere more so than among the acculturated communities of Germany and Austria. Orthodox and Reform rabbis, otherwise so bitterly at odds, were united at least in condemnation of a hare-brained scheme that threatened all the hard-won achievements of social integration. Walter Rathenau coldly rejected Herzl's blandishments to win him over. 'The Jews are no longer a nation and will never become one,' he replied. Ludwig Geiger, a renowned Goethe scholar, was not even sympathetic to helping Russian Jews settle in Palestine. He felt no more for them, he said, than for hungry German day labourers. The neo-Kantian philosopher Hermann

Cohen, on being told that Zionism's aim was to produce a happy new breed of Jews, replied sardonically: 'Aha! So they want to be happy now, do they?' A lifelong critic of Zionism as a reactionary movement, Cohen's opinion was that the Jewish mission was 'to go living among the nations as the God-sent dew, to remain with them and be fruitful for them'.

At the turn of the century, only some four hundred of Germany's half-million Jews had registered as Zionists. The number had risen to six thousand by 1904 but most of them were recently arrived immigrants from eastern Europe. In Hanover, where large numbers of Polish and Russian Jews had settled, the terms '*Ostjude*' and '*Zionist*' were considered interchangeable and equally unacceptable socially. Local Zionist associations were known derisively as '*minyan* clubs', from the ten men required to make up a Jewish prayer quorum.

In the turbulent aftermath of defeat in the First World War, in which Germany's cause had been ardently supported by almost all of its Jews, with notable exceptions such as Einstein, Freud, Karl Popper, the playwright Arthur Schnitzler and the polemical critic Karl Krauss, membership in the German Zionist Federation actually increased, especially after the assassinations of Kurt Eisner, the Jewish first president of the revolutionary Bavarian Republic in 1919, and Foreign Minister Walter Rathenau by anti-Semites in 1922. But, from a peak of 33,000 in 1923, the Zionist Federation's numbers declined to 17,000 in 1929. The Republic appeared to be well established and Jews were playing a self-confident, leading role in the political, cultural, academic and economic life of Weimar's pluralist democracy, open to all talents.

Of those who claimed to be Zionists, less than a third bothered to vote in Zionist elections. At best, they were lukewarm sympathisers, philanthropically concerned to resettle east European Jews in Palestine and typified by the distinguished economist Franz Oppenheimer, who described his cultural make-up as '99% Kant and Goethe and 1% Old Testament via Spinoza and Luther's translation of the Bible'. The symbiosis of Judaism and Germanism through the pursuit of *Bildung*, first mooted by Moses Mendelssohn one hundred and fifty years previously, was reaching its apotheosis.

German Jewry's indifference to Zionism was mirrored by communities elsewhere in Europe and the USA. In democratic countries, the Jews had taken spectacular advantage of emancipation's opportunities; even in the communist USSR, their status had improved beyond recognition since the 1917 Revolution. It was as though the Diaspora philosophy of perseverance and adaptability had finally been validated.

There were approximately sixteen million Jews worldwide in 1930. According to the first census of the British Mandate Administration in 1922, 84,000 lived in Palestine, where the Arab riots of 1921 were followed by a larger uprising in 1929. On the one hand, there was a Diaspora reality of increasing social acceptance, civic equality and shared Enlightenment principles in broadly liberal Western societies; on the other hand, there was a Palestinian reality of a beleaguered, ethnocentric community striving to establish its European socialist blueprint in a hostile Eastern environment. It was a clash of values between two disparate ideologies of the Jewish role in the world – one outward-looking, universal, stressing the commonality between Jews and other peoples; the other inward-looking, particular, accentuating Jewish uniqueness and the historic necessity of self-reliance.

It is instructive to see how this clash of values manifested itself even within the confines of *Yishuv* society and a quixotic attempt to reach an accord with the Arabs.

13 LIBERAL VALUES AND POLITICAL REALITIES

The Council of the League of Nations met in London in July 1922 and confirmed Britain's responsibility for administering Palestinian affairs under the terms of the Palestine Mandate. According to Article II, the mandatory power should place the country under such political, administrative and economic conditions as would secure the establishment of the Jewish national home and the development of self-governing institutions, in fulfilment of the 1917 Balfour Declaration, while safeguarding the civil and religious rights of *all* Palestinians. Article VI required the administration, in cooperation with the Jewish Agency, to facilitate immigration and 'close settlement by Jews of the land.' The stage had been set for the inevitable clash with Palestine's large Arab majority.

During the 1920s, Jewish immigration increased significantly, although, as Robert Weltsch, a delegate to the Zionist Executive and editor of the journal of the German Zionist movement, *Jüdische Rundschau*, pointed out in 1925, even if the current rate of immigration were maintained annually, it would take another forty years before the Jews constituted fifty-one per cent of the population. In microcosm, though, the make-up of those coming to Palestine as part of the Third *Aliyah* (1919–1923), the Fourth *Aliyah* (1924–1928) and the Fifth *Aliyah* (1929–1939) reflected the wider struggle going on in Europe between the ideologies of Communism on the left and Fascism on the right.

The Third *Aliyah* comprised approximately 35,000 immigrants, influenced for the most part by Marxism and radical Socialism. The Fourth *Aliyah* of 60–80,000 immigrants was predominantly middle-class and mainly from Poland. The Fifth *Aliyah*, by far the largest, brought 230,000 immigrants to Palestine who were fleeing the spread of European anti-Semitism prompted by the rise of Nazism.

Like all immigrants to a new land, they came for a variety of reasons, noble or prosaic, and were either motivated by or responding to conditions in the country of their origin. The Third *Aliyah* settlers extended the communal and cooperative goals of their pioneering Russian forebears, founding a General Federation of Trade Unions (*Histadrut*) in 1920, establishing new kibbutzim and promoting the egalitarian principles of Labour Zionism through the manifestos of left-wing political parties. The petit-bourgeois influx of the Fourth *Aliyah*, on the other hand, was prompted by worsening economic conditions in the independent state of Poland created after the First World War, as Jews there were squeezed out of trades, handicrafts and industry. The aspirations of these urban immigrants were represented by the ultra-nationalist, right-wing Revisionist Party, founded in 1925 by Vladimir Jabotinsky.

The immigrants from Germany were distinctive among the class warriors of left and right and few in number by comparison, but wielded a disproportionate intellectual and cultural influence. Before 1933, fewer than two thousand German Jews had settled in Palestine. A mass exodus of German Jewry's intellectual and scientific elite followed the promulgation of Hitler's Nuremberg Laws; of the 118,000 Jews who fled Germany, almost one-third chose Palestine. They were, as one of their number ruefully conceded, a 'difficult export article'. Arriving with elegant furniture and the rare luxury of electric refrigerators, they were unprepared for the harshness of life in Palestine. The joke was that, on the building sites of Tel Aviv, as the buckets full of cement were passed from hand to hand, the labourers would murmur, '*Danke, Herr Doktor. Bitte, Herr Doktor.*'

They came, too, with the liberal values of *Bildung*, at a time when they were being discarded in Europe. Growing support for totalitarianism, whether of the communist or the fascist variety, was finding its echo among Zionists. Idealistic humanists from the German educational system – 'all those Arthurs, Hugos and Hanses', in the sneer of one critic – represented a wan flicker of hope about reaching a peaceful accommodation with the Arabs, before it was snuffed out by the forces on both sides preparing for confrontation.

More warmly welcomed than their political views were the technical and administrative expertise of men such as Arthur Ruppin, who earned the soubriquet of 'Father of Zionist Settlement' and until his death in 1943 was chiefly responsible for the purchase of land and the systematic expansion of the settlement policy in Palestine, and Jacob Thon, his faithful lieutenant in the Jewish Agency, as well as the intellectual lustre of Hugo Bergmann, Martin Buber, Ernst Simon and Gershom Scholem, all faculty members of the Hebrew University. Berl Katznelson, a veteran trade union leader, scoffed that they cared more about the Arabs than Jewish national interests. When Albert Einstein, one of their sympathisers, complained that the Zionists were not doing enough to seek an agreement with the Arabs and cited multinational Switzerland as representing a 'higher stage of political development than any other nation state', Chaim Weizmann, leader of the World Zionist Organisation, responded that Einstein was behaving like a prima donna about to lose her voice.

The association founded by these mainly German-born or German-educated proponents of bi-nationalism as the only proper solution to a conflict between two peoples claiming the same land was called *Brit Shalom* (Covenant of Peace). It never numbered more than two hundred supporters, albeit some of the most illustrious names in the *Yishuv* community, with no popular base or organisational framework, uncertain whether its role should be study and research or active political involvement, whether to cooperate with the official Zionist leadership or to function independently. The brief flowering and slow demise of *Brit Shalom* serves as a handy metaphor for the wider fate of political liberalism in the first half of the twentieth century.

The founders of *Brit Shalom* set out their credo in their first publication, *Sh'ifoteinu* (*Our Aspirations*), issued in Jerusalem in 1927. They wished to create in Palestine 'a bi-national state, in which the two peoples will enjoy totally equal rights as befits the two elements shaping the country's destiny, irrespective of which of the two is numerically superior at any given time'. Their goal was to establish for the Jews of Palestine 'a firm and healthy community which will consist of Jews in as large a number as possible, regardless of whether thereby the Jews will become the majority ... since the question of the majority in the country should in no way be connected to any advantage in rights'.

David Ben-Gurion, in particular, pounced upon the opacity of this formula and demolished it when a delegation from *Brit Shalom* went to discuss bi-nationalism with him in his capacity as a leading figure on the Zionist executive. 'The formula you have proposed does not say anything. It only confuses and therefore damages us, without giving anything to the Arabs. Is it not sufficient that we have one formula, "national home", the meaning of which no one knows, without you adding a second formula which says nothing?'

There, in a nutshell, was the contrast between Zionist nationalism and Diaspora universalism. The high-minded humanists of *Brit Shalom* were unwilling to sully their ideals by political engagement. They debated in the groves of academe, their ethical symposium conducted by Judah Magnes, an American Reform rabbi and first chancellor of the Hebrew University who was a consistently courageous spokesman of bi-nationalism, whereas Ben-Gurion and his pragmatic executive colleagues were perfectly ready to employ morally dubious means towards achieving the end of Jewish statehood. In an influential 1918 essay, *Politics as a Vocation*, Max Weber had argued that in political affairs it was emphatically *not* the case that good could only follow from good and evil only from evil. Often the opposite was true. 'Anyone who fails to see this is, indeed, a political infant.'[1] Ben-Gurion and those around him had grown to political maturity and put away the childish things of their idealist, socialist-imbued youth. They knew by now that, as a disillusioned Arthur Ruppin expressed in a letter to a colleague, 'What we can get [from the Arabs] is of no use to us and what we need we cannot get from them.'

It was the issue of a Legislative Council, proposed by the British, which split *Brit Shalom*. Hugo Bergmann, Judah Magnes and others were pressing for elections to an

Arab–Jewish representative assembly, whereas Ruppin, the organisation's president, was opposed. He predicted that a clash of interests over land acquisition, the introduction of Jewish-only labour and the wage differential between Jewish and Arab workers would combine to ensure that the Arabs would use their constitutional rights to block the economic development of the Jewish minority. Furthermore, he doubted whether 'one can immediately apply to Palestine the principles of democracy ... As long as the majority of Arabs remain illiterate, the crowds will blindly follow a few leaders.'[2] Finally, he feared that, if *Brit Shalom* entered the political arena, 'it will lose its good name for ever'. This happened anyway after the Arab riots of August 1929, in which 133 Jews were killed and hundreds wounded, with even larger casualties on the Arab side. Jewish grief and anger was vented on the naïve advocates of bi-nationalism.

Judah Magnes, brave to the point of foolhardiness, still pressed ahead with the Legislative Council proposal, arguing that the way to train a people in self-government was to place responsibility on the Arabs, not withhold it, and answering the question, whether the 'butchers of Hebron and Safed' should be rewarded by replying, 'Are my own hands clean of blood? [...] Let at least Israel not be hypocritical and self-righteous.'

This was too much for Ruppin. He felt obliged to resign the presidency of *Brit Shalom*, citing irresponsible pronouncements without adequate preparation of the Jewish public and stating that 'the Arabs interpret our conciliatory tone as weakness'. That, effectively, spelt the end of *Brit Shalom*. Ruppin, his prestige severely dented, was eventually replaced in the settlement department of the Jewish Agency, having performed one last service for the *Yishuv*; helping to negotiate an arrangement with the Hitler government whereby the large-scale immigration of German Jews between 1933 and 1935 was made possible.

The constant tension between trying to uphold moral principles while pursuing an aggressive settlement policy in a country of hostile natives was a circle that Ruppin could not square. After an early *Brit Shalom* meeting, he confided in his diary: 'In general, it has become clear how difficult it is to realise Zionism while constantly adapting it to ethical demands. Has Zionism in fact deteriorated to pointless chauvinism?'[3] A letter written in March 1936 to Robert Weltsch, a fellow German and *Brit Shalom* co-founder, revealed the extent to which *Bildung* idealism had been corroded by political exigencies: 'Not negotiations, but the development of Palestine towards a larger percentage of Jews in the population, and a strengthening of our economic position, can and will bring about an easing of tension ... When coming to an understanding with us will no longer mean that the Arabs have to make concessions to us, but only a question of coming to terms with realities ... we are living in a latent state of war with the Arabs that makes loss of life inevitable ... If we want to continue our work in Palestine, we will have to accept such losses.'

In his younger days, Ruppin had been a proto-communist. 'I could not imagine a higher aim than to be working in Russia now on the peaceful reorganisation of that country' is a diary entry in 1921. 'I very much respect the magnificent ideas inherent in Bolshevism.' Two years later he was optimistic that 'a new and more just social order will issue from Palestine'. That required practical cooperation with the Arabs. 'I think that I shall not be able to continue working for the Zionist movement if Zionism does not acquire a new theoretical foundation. Herzl's conception of the Jewish state was possible only because he ignored the existence of the Arabs [an allusion, perhaps, to Herzl's favourite evocation of "a land without a people for a people without a land", and the apocryphal story that Max Nordau, one of his most ardent supporters, had gone to him in despair and exclaimed, "But you never told us that Arabs are living there. We are doing them a great injustice!"] [...] Zionism can find its justification only in racial affiliation of the Jews to the peoples of the Near East. [...] What continually worries me is the relationship between Jews and Arabs in Palestine. [...] I have no doubt that Zionism will end in catastrophe if we do not succeed in finding a common platform.'

Yet, within a decade, Ruppin had veered to pessimistic acceptance of an unavoidable conflagration. His personal disillusion and the trajectory of his thinking, from confidence in an Arab–Jewish partnership to bitter recognition that it was unobtainable, serve to illustrate a more general divide that had opened up between Diaspora idealism and Zionist *realpolitik*, between the old values emphasised by over two thousand years of political powerlessness and the new realities required to achieve power and bring into being the first Jewish state for two thousand years.

14 ZIONISM'S RADICAL DEMANDS

It is a galling irony that, between them, Hitler and his National Socialist German Workers' (Nazi) Party did more in ten years to accelerate the creation of a Jewish state than all of Zionist endeavour had managed in the previous fifty. The steady erosion of non-Aryan civil rights between 1933 and 1935, culminating in the Nuremberg Laws depriving Jews of the vote, forbidding marriage or sexual relations between Jews and Aryans and defining a Jew as anyone who had a Jewish grandparent, shattered the Enlightenment vision of citizens of different faiths living together in amiable accord under a benign civil authority. Nazi ideology was an atavistic throwback to mediaeval prejudice, bigotry and religious persecution.

The great weakness of those who proclaim 'reason' as their guide is that they rarely take into account the power of the irrational. Rational people in Germany, including most Jews, failed to imagine the consequences of what Hitler so openly preached or that a civilised country steeped in *Bildung* values would tolerate this vulgar Austrian demagogue as more than a passing aberration. By the time they awoke to reality, it was too late to wish that they had listened to the warnings of Carl Jung, himself no friend of the Jews, that Hitler was the mystic medicine man, incarnating the worst fantasies of the German collective unconscious. Sophisticated Germans were not the only ones not to take Hitler seriously, at least initially. It was an oft-remarked curiosity that this man, who had Germany in his thrall, left most foreigners distinctly unimpressed.

In September 1935, the same month in which the Nuremberg Laws were promulgated, the maverick outsider Vladimir Jabotinsky founded his breakaway New Zionist Organisation. He boasted that 713,000 votes had been cast for his delegates, against a total of 1.2 million subscribers claimed by the World Zionist Organisation. It is safe to assume that both sets of figures were generously inflated, which goes to show what a minority following Zionism still had among world Jewry, even after Hitler's rise to power. The evidence of acceptance and acculturation in Western democracies, occasional flurries of anti-Semitism notwithstanding, was more appealing to most Jews than the prospect of nation-building in a hostile Middle East. The overwhelming majority of those who paid their *shekel* membership fee to the World Zionist Organisation were doing so in the time-honoured fashion of one Jew collecting money from a second Jew in order to send a third Jew to Palestine. After two thousand years without a homeland, the Diaspora appeared to have been validated as the normative form of Jewish existence. Universalism rather than nationalism was the prevailing Jewish Zeitgeist.

In Palestine itself, the influx of refugees from Hitler's Germany had exacerbated the worsening situation between Arabs and Jews. Soon it would escalate into the Arab Revolt of

1936 to 1939. By now, everyone in the Zionist leadership privately recognised that war with the Arabs was inevitable, even while officially talking the language of accommodation and going through the motions of negotiating with the Mandate government about immigration quotas, land purchase and equal representation in a legislative chamber. Since the 1929 disturbances, Ben-Gurion had been keeping a confidential tally of the manpower potential of neighbouring Arab states in the event of war.

Throughout the 1930s, the self-absorbed *Yishuv* was preoccupied with three main issues, in descending order of importance: its relationship with the British Mandate; the intense rivalry between the Mapai Party, which comprised most of the leadership of socialist Zionism, and Jabotinsky's Revisionist Party; and how to deal with the Arabs. Only one man had the prescience to look up from this navel-gazing and foresee the stages of a forthcoming European conflagration. Writing to Jewish Agency colleagues in January 1935, David Ben-Gurion, its chairman, predicted that 'the disaster which has befallen German Jewry is not limited to Germany alone'. Hitler's regime placed the entire Jewish people in danger. He could not survive without a war of revenge against France, Poland, Czechoslovakia and Soviet Russia. 'The Jewish people are not a world factor with the ability to prevent or delay this danger or to weaken or diminish it.' Nevertheless, in one tiny corner of the world, the Jews were a principle factor, if not yet the decisive one. What would be their significance 'on the day of judgement, when the great world disaster will begin? Who knows, perhaps only four or five years, if not less, stand between us and that awful day.'

By contrast, his obdurate rival Jabotinsky, who, perversely, proclaimed himself an upholder of the great ideals of nineteenth-century liberalism while founding a party and youth movement that were proto-fascist, was convinced right up until September 1939 that there would be no war. A cosmopolitan European, fluent in several languages with Italy his spiritual home, Jabotinsky aroused the suspicions of provincial, Marxist-imbued, fellow Russian Zionists precisely on account of his sophisticated airs and familiarity with wider culture. He, too, refused to imagine that European civilisation could succumb to Nazi barbarism, once dismissing his hero-worshipping acolyte and successor, Menachem Begin, with the stinging rebuke that if he no longer believed in 'the conscience of the world', then he should go drown himself in the Vistula.

It is important to remember that, before the Second World War, the last major involvement of the British government in Palestine was to issue the MacDonald White Paper in May 1939. Effectively, it abrogated the Balfour Declaration and terminated the Mandate. Despite the parlous and well-publicised plight of German and Austrian Jewish refugees expelled by Hitler or interned in concentration camps and recent, vivid memories of the November 1938 *Kristallnacht* (Night of broken glass) pogrom, the White Paper proposed limiting Jewish immigration to a total of 75,000 newcomers over the next five years and thereafter subject to Arab consent, the curtailment of land sales and Arab self-government with autonomous authority for the Jewish minority.

The proposals were rejected by Jews and Arabs alike. The permanent Mandates Commission of the League of Nations expressed the view that the White Paper was in breach of the provisions of the Palestine Mandate. Before the British government could present its case in September 1939, war had begun. Ben-Gurion summed up the Zionist response to the outbreak of hostilities with a pithy slogan: the *Yishuv* would fight the war against Hitler as if there were no White Paper and would fight the White Paper as if there were no war against Hitler. As never before, the future of the Zionist community in Palestine had been catapulted to the forefront of Jewish consciousness, in the perennial fashion of Jewish history, due less to its own volition than to the pressure on it of more powerful external forces.

The Holocaust, during which approximately 6.1 million of Europe's Jews were gassed, murdered, starved to death or driven to suicide, appeared to validate conclusively Zionism's central tenet that, without a homeland of their own, the powerless Jewish people were perpetually destined to be at the whim of nations among whom they lived. The Nazi extermination programme was simply the culmination, albeit on a vaster and industrial scale, of centuries of anti-Semitism.

In refurbishing the mediaeval symbols of oppression, the Nazis gave credence to this Zionist reading of Jewish history. They repealed the citizenship of Germany's Jews, thereby revoking the gains of emancipation. They forced the Jews out of the professions and the arts, thereby repudiating their integration into wider society. They compelled all Jews to wear the yellow star, thereby signifying their segregation. In territories they conquered, they forced the Jews into ghettos, the word most redolent of past persecution and *untermensch* status.

The magnitude of European Jewry's destruction was greater than anyone, Zionist or otherwise, could begin to imagine. By the end of 1942, word had reached Palestine that a systematic extermination programme was being implemented, and the American State Department confirmed that two million Jews had already perished. Chaim Weizmann estimated privately that twenty-five per cent of central European Jewry would not survive under German occupation; in the event, it was nearer to seventy per cent.

Partial knowledge of the massacres being perpetrated against European Jewry prompted six hundred American Zionists meeting at the Biltmore Hotel in New York in May 1942 to issue recommendations more radical than anything previously adopted at Zionist conferences. Calling for the fulfilment of the Balfour Declaration's 'original purpose' and repudiating the 1939 White Paper, the delegates passed a resolution calling for a Jewish 'commonwealth' to be established in the *whole* of Palestine as part of the new world order after the defeat of Fascism. They generously conceded minority rights for the large Arab majority in the proposed new commonwealth.

Until now, it had been more prudent to express the end goal of Zionism in euphemisms such as 'Jewish homeland' or 'national home'. Any public discussion of statehood was a taboo subject among the official Zionist leadership, which placed its strategic hopes in cooperation with the British. Only someone such as Jabotinsky, in permanent opposition to the Jewish Agency, could openly express ultimate aims with the candid simplicity of his Revisionist Party's first manifesto of April 1925. 'The aim of Zionism is a Jewish state. The territory – both sides of the Jordan. The system – mass colonisation. The solution of the financial problem – a national loan...' The opening two sentences of that manifesto, incidentally, became the shibboleth of the Revisionist Party and then its successor, the Likud Party, much as Clause Four about public ownership of the means of production was for the British Labour Party. Unlike Clause Four, however, it has never been repealed, a fact which international statesmen and diplomats should bear in mind whenever a Likud government is in power, as they try to find a way out of the quagmire of Israeli–Palestinian relations.

Six months later, the Zionist Actions Committee adopted the Biltmore Programme as official policy, a victory for Revisionism even though it languished politically in Palestine and abroad. The World Zionist Congress of September 1945, meeting in London for the first time after the war, endorsed an even bolder resolution, previously adopted unanimously by American Zionists, calling for a 'free and democratic Jewish Commonwealth ... [which] shall embrace the whole of Palestine, undivided and undiminished'.

David Ben-Gurion, the prime minister-in-waiting, had been at the forefront of those encouraging the more militant stance of American Zionism. He was willing to steal Revisionism's clothes if it furthered his Second World War policy of steadfastly pursuing two consistent yet divergent strategies; on the one hand, a diplomatic reorientation away from Britain towards America, the superpower, whose six million-strong Jewish community would provide crucial support in post-war lobbying for Jewish statehood; on the other hand, active partnership with the Mandate authorities in the war effort, even to the extent of handing over Revisionist terrorists and sympathisers, insofar as it strengthened the institutions of the *Yishuv* and developed the capabilities of its fledgling army, the *Haganah*, for future confrontation with the Arabs. It was a transformation not lost on Ben-Gurion's allies and opponents alike that this former small-town Marxist from Poland should have sought so ardently the embraces of the most capitalist nation on the planet. But, as a young man, Ben-Gurion had listened to and been impressed by Lenin. What he particularly admired was that 'before him he sees one direction, that which leads to his goal, and he turns neither left nor right, whilst he remains ready to use different routes as the situation demands. For he pursues one path – to his goal.'[1]

For Ben-Gurion, the goal of Zionism, *tout court*, was a Jewish state. A few eminent Jews, such as Hannah Arendt, Albert Einstein, Martin Buber and Leo Baeck (all, significantly, the products of a German *Bildung* education) publicly expressed their reservations in open letters to *The New York Times* and elsewhere, wanly reiterating their belief in an understanding between the two peoples in Palestine, but theirs were lonely voices. Stunned and horrified by the evidence from the concentration camps and desperate to find a refuge in Palestine for the 250,000 Holocaust survivors languishing in European displaced persons' camps, the overwhelming bulk of world Jewry endorsed every effort to achieve statehood. The Zionist leadership could have been excused for triumphantly exclaiming, 'We are all Zionists now!'

However, unlike fantasists in the Revisionist Party who had initiated terrorist attacks against British military personnel and Arab civilians, Ben-Gurion was keenly aware of the limitations on Jewish freedom to act unilaterally and how dependent the new state would be on Big Power patronage. He understood the geopolitical constraints under which the First and Second Jewish commonwealths had survived in the biblical past and would have to do so in the future.

15 HOLOCAUST SURVIVORS AND ZIONIST INCOMPREHENSION

Somewhere in *The Catcher in the Rye*, that seminal text for generations of angst-ridden adolescents, Holden Caulfield has quoted to him the observation of psychoanalyst Wilhelm Stenkel that the mark of an immature man is that he wants to die nobly for a cause, while the mark of the mature man is that he wants to live humbly for one.

Zionism in its formative years, especially in the Revisionist version, had a distinctive predilection for the epics of noble failure in the Jewish past rather than tales of humble fortitude. The Greek writer George Seferis coined the useful word 'mythistory' to describe those collective memories of a people that are part-reality, part-fancy. In Zionist mythistory, the factually dubious account by Josephus of 960 besieged defenders at Masada preferring mass suicide to falling into the hands of the Romans, an event that had been played down in Jewish collective memory for almost two thousand years, was deemed more relevant and inspirationally potent than

Rabbinic Judaism's preference for Rabbi Yohanan ben Zakkai, whose establishment, with Roman consent, of the academy at Yavneh had enabled sacred study to continue even after military disaster. During the years of embryonic state-building, members of the *Yishuv*'s elite military corps, the *Palmach*, climaxed their training with an arduous ascent to Masada's peak, where they would swear an oath to nation and homeland, vowing, in the words of Isaac Lamdan's 1927 poem, that 'Masada will not fall again'. Youth movements quickly grasped the symbolism of a march to Masada and it became a form of military preparation, the young hikers undertaking a week-long exploration through the desert, equipped with pistol, climbing ropes, heavy packs of food and clothing, sleeping bags, musical instruments, maps and Bibles. Once the state had been established and during Moshe Dayan's term as chief of staff in the 1950s, the climb to Masada's peak became the central feature of the swearing-in of army recruits. They would ascend the winding trail in a long column for a night-time ceremony by torchlight.

A recent failure that was appropriated for its mythistorical potential was the death in 1920 of Joseph Trumpeldor and six comrades while vainly defending the isolated settlement of Tel Chai in Upper Galilee against Arab marauders. According to accounts that were circulated immediately afterwards, Trumpeldor's last words were, 'It is good to die for our country.' The scene of a mortally wounded patriot dedicating his life for a higher cause would have been irresistible to Verdi, which is certainly how Jabotinsky, an avid fan of flags, uniforms, parades and all things operatic, utilised it. He named his Zionist youth movement *Betar*, an acronym of *Brit Trumpeldor* (Covenant of Trumpeldor), a felicitous play on words, because *Betar* also happened to be the place name of the last, futile stand by Bar Kochba and his rebels against Roman rule in AD 135 – two instances of heroic martyrdom for the price of one. It was an example of historical revisionism conveniently overlooked by Jabotinsky that he had been opposed to sending help to Tel Chai because he did not approve of piecemeal colonising.

A memorial in the shape of a roaring lion was erected at Tel Chai. Youth movements would hike there, turning it into a site of pilgrimage and dedication. An educational ritual of drama and song developed at the memorial, to symbolise the Zionist values of settlement-building, armed bravery, comradeship and pioneering love of the Holy Land. It was one more inspirational example, and a contemporary one, to add to the 'few against the many' motif that Zionism emphasised in Jewish history, whether the Exodus from Egypt, David versus Goliath or the Maccabees defeating the Syrian Hellenists.

Every new religious or political movement needs to validate itself by stressing that it is a continuation and fulfilment of, not a rupture with, the past. Zionism was no different, sifting the images of Jewish history and making use of those that most suited its self-understanding and self-representation. The soldier was more relevant to its purposes than the scholar, the man of action rather than the philosopher. Among Zionist youth, simple, straight talk was prized above abstract theorising. The upright, candid virtues of the pioneer-farmer, a latter-day cowboy hero, were preferred to the intellectual qualifications and hesitations characteristic of the *yeshivah* student, therefore of Diaspora ignominy.

The sharp distinction drawn by Zionism between the Diaspora Jew and his Palestinian counterpart, the 'new Hebrew', was made manifest in the response to Holocaust survivors. Although the *Yishuv* was shocked at reports of the massacre of millions of European Jews, there was a hint of retrospective validation in its reaction. Yitzchak Tabenkin, a leader of the kibbutz movement, told a council meeting in July 1943: 'These times have once more shown, in a terrible light, the fundamental truth of Zionism, which is the Jewish person cannot exist in the Diaspora.' At a youth convention in the same year, he opined that, had Diaspora Jews been taught to stand upright in the manner of Zionists, 'perhaps they would have changed something, saved something, at least their honour and self-worth'.

A concomitant anxiety was that, far from 'vindicating' Zionism, the scale of the Holocaust would deprive the movement of its *raison d'être*. Zionism's main argument had always been that east Europe's millions of Jews needed and yearned for a homeland in Palestine. The loss of six million rendered that argument redundant. In a private letter, Chaim Weizmann feared that, without this critical mass, demands for a state 'based on the imperative necessity of transferring large numbers of Jews speedily to Palestine will ... fall to the ground'.[1] David Ben-Gurion confessed to a 'terrifying vision' that gave him sleepless nights: 'The extermination of European Jewry meant the end of Zionism, for there will be no one to build Palestine.'[2]

Years of Zionist education denigrating Diaspora existence spawned complicated, sometimes extreme, responses to Holocaust victims. The vast majority were judged to have gone passively to their fate, 'like lambs to the slaughter'. Zionist youth, in contrast, would have risen up against their oppressors. It caused Moshe Tabenkin, a youth leader in Palestine, to confess that, for him, 'rejection of the Diaspora ... now turned into personal hatred of the Diaspora. I hate it as a man hates a deformity he is ashamed of.'[3]

Yishuv sympathy for Holocaust survivors was tempered by the explicit assumption that they were the products of what one American journalist called 'a kind of grim, perverted Darwinism, psychologically and physically'.[4] Those who had 'perished' (the standard Hebrew description for Jews killed in the Holocaust, whereas Jews who died fighting in Palestine were said to have 'fallen') in the camps had been the more refined elements; the 'fittest' (i.e. the most adaptable) had survived through cunning, toughness and selfishness – or collaboration. This process of reverse natural selection was bringing the least desirable remnant of European Jewry to Palestine. 'A mixed multitude of human dust without a language, without education, without roots and without any roots in the nation's tradition and vision' is how Ben-Gurion described them. 'Turning these people of dust into a cultured, independent nation with a vision will be no easy task.'[5]

'Human dust', a phrase coined in the 1930s by the Zionist writer David Frishman to connote the spineless masses of east European Jewry blown hither and thither by the wind, was the standard label of the *Yishuv* leadership for Holocaust survivors. Other commonplace terms used by the tough, no-nonsense, Palestinian-born *Sabra* generations were *agadim*, from the Hebrew initials for 'people of the mournful Diaspora', and *sabonim*, 'bars of soap', a supposedly humorous allusion to the rumour that the Nazis turned the bodies of their victims into soap.

The only elements of perished European Jewry that escaped exasperated Zionist incomprehension were the partisans or the Warsaw Ghetto rebels. At least they died with guns in their hands. The fact that many of these fighters had belonged to Zionist youth movements in the countries of their annihilation forged an empathetic bond. They had fought back, acted differently from the passive majority, thanks to the Zionist values they had embraced. In popular mythology, they were linked with Trumpeldor and other *Yishuv* heroes such as Enzo Sereni and Hannah Szenes, who had parachuted into occupied Europe to aid them.

The innate assumption that the condition of Diaspora Jewry was morally and physically inferior to that of the healthy, new Hebrew was given tangible corroboration by the pitiful state in which survivors arrived in Palestine, suffering from disease, malnutrition and mental trauma. From a pre-war background that had been mainly urban, capitalist or religion-centred, younger survivors were catapulted into the socialist collectivity of the kibbutzim and the secular ethos of the army, gearing up for war with the Arabs. The transition was painful, usually accompanied by peer group hostility, social exclusion or patronising condescension towards an inferior, as the many subsequent testimonies of these compulsory immigrants make clear.[6]

Yet they were, *faute de mieux*, the uprooted human resource which gave urgency to Zionism's call for Mandate immigration quotas to be lifted, the raw material making imperative a Jewish state. Unimpressed though he was with the calibre of the 'surviving remnant', Ben-Gurion was ready to turn their tragedy to advantage. 'Disaster is strength if channelled to a productive course,' he told the Zionist Executive as early as October 1942. 'The whole trick of Zionism is that it knows how to channel our disaster, not into despondency or degradation, as is the case in the Diaspora, but into a source of creativity and exploitation'[7] – which is precisely what he did.

Nowadays, it is axiomatic to see a causal connection between the Holocaust and the establishment of the State of

Israel a mere three years later. The standard version is that the Western world's guilt over its inaction before and during the Holocaust impelled the major powers to vote for Israel's creation. Typical of such received wisdom is the statement by one writer that the Western world 'voted in late 1947 to give the Jews their own state as partial remittance for its complicity in the Nazi Holocaust'.[8] Another study claimed that 'the leadership of the Western world, especially in America, could not escape the guilt. A shamefaced, remorseful post-war West now supported the Jewish demand for an independent state in Palestine.'[9] Even so painstaking and voluminous a chronicler of the Holocaust as Yehuda Bauer makes the startling generalisation that American troops, having fought their way across France and Germany, were stricken with guilt 'when they realised how little the free world had done to avert the Holocaust'.[10] Among numerous similar assertions, this author must confess his own contribution in a book on Zionist ideology that 'a guilty world sanctioned [the Jewish state] into being more speedily than it otherwise would have done, as atonement for its indifference to the Nazi death camps'.[11]

In fact, recent research, notably by the historian Peter Novick in his indispensable *The Holocaust and Collective Memory*, has demonstrated conclusively that any linkage between one event and the other is more fanciful than real. There is no evidence that any of the nations who voted by thirty-three votes to thirteen at the United Nations on 29 November 1947 to partition Palestine between the Arabs and the Jews, were prompted by 'guilt'. America and the crucial Soviet bloc, who together orchestrated the resolution, had concrete interests and geopolitical strategy at the forefront of their considerations. The Soviet Union wanted to loosen British power in the Middle East and gain its own foothold there. The Truman administration was conscious of the influential American–Jewish vote in the forthcoming election. Latin American countries, which supplied the lion's share of the favourable votes, were far removed from involvement or implication in the European catastrophe but keenly aware of their military and economic reliance on their neighbour to the north. David Vital, the foremost historian of Zionism, has dismissed as 'absurd' the notion that 'modern Israel resulted from, was, so to speak, born of, the Holocaust – perhaps as a bone thrown to the unfortunates by belatedly and guiltily benevolent powers as compensation for miseries suffered. Nothing could be further from the truth, as even a superficial examination of British and American policy in the immediate post-war period will show.'[12]

All this notwithstanding, spontaneous sympathy for the Holocaust survivors (two-thirds of whom, some 160,000 people, arrived in Palestine) undoubtedly disposed non-committed observers to look positively on Jewish aspirations for statehood. In the free world's largest, most prosperous repository of Jews, the United States, efforts to aid refugees and lobby for statehood galvanised all but the negligible ultra-Orthodox and secularly unaffiliated minorities. Not to declare oneself a Zionist was akin to being involved in un-American activities.

In a little over fifty years, Zionism, the newcomer among Jewish responses to modernity, had imposed itself over more than two thousand years of Diaspora experience. But in keeping with the lessons of Jewish history, it owed its success more to powerlessness than power, to the vagaries of alliances between the mighty rather than to its own scope for independent action.

16 FROM DESTRUCTION IN EUROPE TO REDEMPTION IN ISRAEL

For the past thirty years, it has been a given in any discussion of international politics that Israel is America's client state, her most valuable and heavily subsidised ally in the Middle East, and that the staunchest advocate of this alliance is the powerful, five million-strong American–Jewish community, whose twin pillars in a 'civil religion' that incorporates almost all of left and right, Republicans and Democrats, religious or secular, are support for Israel and memorialising the Holocaust.

It is hard to remember a time when this was not the case, but, during the first twenty years of Israel's existence, a different reality applied. Nowadays, it is de rigueur for every self-respecting metropolis in the United States to have its own Holocaust memorial or museum. Europe, where the catastrophe occurred, is noticeably more reticent in commemorating the Holocaust. *The Diary of Anne Frank* and the life of its Jewish heroine have been successfully universalised by churches and educationalists to teach lessons about mutual responsibility, the crime of genocide and racial awareness. But, in the aftermath of the Second World War, those who survived Nazi extermination camps really were 'the Jews of Silence'. Whether fortunate enough to make it to their first choice of America or being absorbed as immigrants in Israel, the survivors were not expected to speak about their experiences. It went against the grain of building a new life, putting the shameful Diaspora past behind them and, in the case of American newcomers, embracing that country's 'can-do' ethos. Therapy was a guilty secret and a stiff upper lip the recommended response to trauma.

Although Ben-Gurion had identified American Jewry as the main reservoir of Diaspora aid for the new state and personally launched the sale of Israeli bonds in the United States, American Jews' donations to Israel steadily declined throughout the years before the Six Day War of 1967. In a study commissioned in the late 1950s in a Midwestern suburb, only twenty-one per cent of respondents listed 'support for Israel' as an essential quality one needed in order to be considered a good Jew, whereas fifty-eight per cent answered 'helping the underprivileged'. Nearly half of those questioned thought that supporting Israel was 'desirable', but thirty-two per cent judged that it made no difference to being a good Jew. When Israel launched its 1956 Sinai campaign in collusion with France and Great Britain, and was forced to withdraw from Sinai by a sharply critical President Eisenhower, American–Jewish lobbying on behalf of Israel was muted; in the election that immediately followed, Eisenhower actually increased his share of the Jewish vote.[1]

The decade of the 1950s afforded Jews an unprecedented opportunity to cement their status in the mainstream of (white) American life. Although it was still possible, especially in the

South, to see signs outside country clubs barring 'Jews, Niggers and Dogs', a booming economy, the feel-good factor from having fought a just war against evil enemies in Europe and the Pacific and the sense of unlimited latent potential in a nation furthering its Manifest Destiny combined to produce a mood of upbeat optimism faithfully reflected in the Hollywood (itself largely a Jewish preserve) movies of the time. A stock-in-trade plot of war films was how an ill-assorted bunch of individuals – the East Side Jew, the Brooklyn Italian, the hill-billy, the Texan cowboy, the bespectacled college type, the Negro and the southern racist – would be moulded into an efficient fighting force by the wise, Abraham-Lincolnesque company commander (regularly played by Jewish Jeff Chandler!), his death in action making the men all the more determined to go forward in unison to victory. The melting pot made an American of everyone.

Hundreds of thousands of Jewish servicemen had fought in the war. Three-quarters of them were second- or third-generation American-born. They came home to take advantage of the GI Bill of Rights and the new social mobility as education, industry and commerce expanded. What Germany had been for Jews in the first three decades of the twentieth century, America now became in the 1950s and 1960s. If anywhere was a national homeland, it was not the tiny State of Israel but the America of suburban Reform temples, affluent Jewish community centres, Rotary and Sisterhood chapters.

Another factor militated against excessive trumpeting of Israel. The former scourge of Nazism had been replaced by the new danger of Soviet Communism. Senator Joe McCarthy was getting into his stride, whipping up hysteria about alien agitators. In Israel, Ben-Gurion had abandoned any pretence of Socialism as he gave priority to the army, immigration and settlement as the staples of state-building, but, for the American public, Communism and Jews had been synonymously suspect since the Bolshevik Revolution. Israel's founding generation was largely the product of that revolution. According to a private FBI estimate in the late 1940s, fifty to sixty per cent of American Communist Party members were Jews. The American–Russian alliance during the Second World War had temporarily muted charges of Jewish philo-Sovietism, but they resurfaced when Jewish names figured in espionage prosecutions, culminating in the controversial trial and execution of Julius and Ethel Rosenberg for spying. The major communal organisations worked desperately to disassociate Jews from the taint of Communist sympathies. Too overt an espousal of Israel's cause would have been impolitic, inviting slurs about dual loyalties. In those years, enamoured of the socialist kibbutzim and Israel's fledgling democracy, the European left was more enthusiastic about the Israeli experiment in state-building than was capitalist American Jewry.

It came as a relief to the Jewish public relations agencies in America when Stalin gave vent to blatant anti-Semitism in the show trial of Joseph Slansky and other Jewish leaders of the Czech Communist Party in 1952 and then in the so-called Doctors' Plot. The chance to paint Communism and Fascism as two sides of the same coin, both being inimical to the Jews, was an opportune propaganda tool. Articles and press releases made explicit connections between Hitler's and Stalin's identical goals for European Jewry. The Russian tyrant wanted to liquidate the remnant left by Hitler. A second extermination was imminent. One fanciful press release put out by the American Jewish Committee alleged that the East German government was rounding up 'non-Aryans' on the basis of Nazi racial laws. Apart from a deluded few who refused to learn, it could be shown that American Jews were as staunchly opposed to Communism as they had been to Fascism, with equally good reason.

It is widely recognised, with the benefit of hindsight, that two events were intrinsic to changing American Jewry's perception of both the Holocaust and the State of Israel. The first was the trial of Adolf Eichmann in Jerusalem in 1961. The second was the Six Day War of 1967.

Despite worldwide interest in the story of Eichmann's capture in Argentina and the attention to detail with which his trial was conducted, its effect was almost the opposite of what its instigators intended and worried bystanders feared. The Israeli government, in asserting moral guardianship of the memory of the six million by bringing a leading perpetrator of the Holocaust to justice, wished thereby to educate the younger generations in their Diaspora history. In presenting the prosecution case, Attorney-General Gideon Hauser hammered home the theme of persistent and endemic anti-Semitism; Eichmann was the most recent, and worst, in a genealogy of anti-Semitic hatred that reached back to Pharaoh in the Bible. Implicit throughout Hauser's lengthy presentation was the Zionist message that only in a country of their own could Jews avoid the vulnerability and persecution of Diaspora existence.

Instead of sympathy for the fate of their grandparents' generation, the widespread reaction of Israeli youth was shame and exasperated incomprehension. Why had they gone like sheep to the slaughter, instead of fighting back as Israelis would have done? Rather than building a bridge of understanding between Israelis and Diaspora Jews, the Eichmann trial accentuated the gulf between their values and reinforced the innate Zionist sense of superiority.

In the United States, on the other hand, where the American Jewish Congress and the Anti-Defamation League had feared that coverage of the trial would exacerbate anti-Semitism by concentrating on the Jew-as-victim stereotype and highlighting Jewish vengefulness in apposition to Christian forgiveness, the anticipated backlash did not occur. Whatever doubts had been expressed, by Jews among others, about the legality of kidnapping Eichmann, they were more than offset by the public perception of plucky Israel taking the fight to erstwhile Nazi persecutors. The image of the tough, self-reliant 'new Jew' gained general currency. That in turn freed American Jews of their inhibitions about discussing the Holocaust. From now on, it would be presented as a uniquely Jewish catastrophe, referring specifically to the annihilation of European Jewry and not, as before, under the heading of widespread Nazi barbarism or the evils of totalitarianism in general.

But, while the Jewish version of all-American baseball player, movie star and corporate man was staking his claim in the United States and the typical cartoon representation of an Israeli was a sturdy *kibbutznik* in shorts and sandals, wider societal and geopolitical considerations, as always, would define either's freedom of manoeuvre. The civil rights movement and deepening involvement in Vietnam became more pressing concerns for American Jews than Israel or memorialising the Holocaust.

In the Middle East, Gamal Abdul Nasser had emerged as the dominant personality. His alliance with the Soviet Union and construction of a Pan-Arab federation to encircle Israel threatened the young state's existence. A stagnating Israeli economy, three years in which emigration had exceeded immigration and a political system in disarray, due to ideological and generational tensions centred on the vendetta

Ben-Gurion was pursuing against his former colleague Pinchas Lavon, appeared further to expose Israel's fragility. Nasser calculated that now was the time to turn the screw.

Appearances and Arab rhetoric to the contrary, no contemporary military analysis suggested that Israel would be defeated on the battlefield. American intelligence estimated that it would take Israel seven to ten days to overrun the combined Egyptian–Syrian armies. More bullish Israeli intelligence thought no longer than a week.[2]

But that was not how it appeared to the outside world when, in May 1967, Nasser closed the Straits of Tiran to Israeli shipping, a deliberate *casus belli*, and expelled United Nations Emergency Force peacekeepers. In public appearances, the Israeli prime minister, Levi Eshkol, was hesitant and out of his depth, and the United Nations waffled ineffectually to find a compromise, in contrast to the photos of a beaming Nasser surrounded by cocky fighter pilots. With Arab propaganda crowing triumphantly that Israel would be wiped off the map and the Zionists driven into the sea, Jews in the Diaspora feared a second Holocaust. That, certainly, was the reaction of this author, a 27-year-old postgraduate student in Dublin, when I went to volunteer. It felt preferable to die fighting alongside one's own people than to survive from afar and go on calling oneself a Jew after two such overwhelming disasters in little more than twenty years. Suddenly, the existential fragility of the Jewish condition, with or without a homeland, was manifest in all its starkness.

Diaspora Jewry mobilised as never before on behalf of Israel, with public rallies, concerted fund-raising and a small army of young volunteers, which in the event was not needed. Rather disappointingly, I arrived on the fourth day of the war, when victory was already assured, just in time to watch from the fields of the kibbutz to which I had been assigned as a Syrian bomber was pursued by two Israeli fighter planes and shot down in a spiralling plume of flame over the Golan Heights. A week after the war began, I was among an estimated 200,000 pilgrims doing a circuit of the walls of Jerusalem on the festival of *Shavuot*, sullenly watched from their windows by the curfewed Palestinian residents of the Old City.

The Six Day War was not quite the surgically precise operation of subsequent propaganda. Like all wars, it had its share of errors in combat, mistaken commands, instances of cowardice and heroism and examples of stubborn resistance by individual Egyptian, Syrian or Jordanian units, not all of whom threw down their weapons and fled as popular legend had it. But the speed, daring and élan of the Israeli advance and the overwhelming scope of the victory lent itself to biblical imagery from the religiously inclined and frequent resort, even by hard-bitten secularists, to use of the adjective 'miraculous'. With a mighty hand, Israel had been delivered from the valley of the shadow and confounded the enemies who had purposed to destroy her. As Jews stood before the one surviving wall of the ancient Temple, under their control for the first time in two thousand years, or made excursions to previously out-of-bounds Jericho and the Tomb of the Patriarchs in Hebron, the heady whiff of Messianism was in the air. Ben-Gurion, the political realist, recommended immediately after the war that the conquered territories should be given back as a preliminary to peace negotiations but Moshe Dayan, the hero of the hour, was despatched to the old man's desert retreat of S'deh Boker to tell him to pipe down.

The transition from a prelude of despair to a finale of exultant triumph marked a permanent shift in the

Israel–Diaspora relationship. Where previously thoughtful commentators, following theologian Leo Baeck's categorisation, had been wont to describe Israel and the Diaspora as two foci of an ellipse, 'the centrality of Israel to Jewish life' now became the standard catchphrase of fund-raisers, sermonising rabbis, youth leaders and candidates for communal office. Delegations flocked to Israel to pledge their unwavering support for the government in its quest for peace and major organisations transferred their headquarters there, preferably to reunified Jerusalem.

At first hesitantly, then with more conviction, a new schema evolved in which Israel's deliverance was seen, if not as recompense, then at least as partial consolation for the enormity of the Holocaust. A causal continuity was established between two landmark events. From destruction in Europe to redemption in the Land of Israel became the axiomatically linked markers for conducting any intellectual or theological dialogue about the future of the Jewish people. A strong Israel was not only the beacon for world Jewry but also the only guarantor of Diaspora survival. By supporting Israel, one ensured that Hitler was not granted a posthumous victory. This conviction intensified six years later, when the early hours of the 1973 Yom Kippur War threatened the very existence of Israel itself.

17 A FALSE SENSE OF SECURITY

Between the Six Day War of June 1967 and the Yom Kippur War of October 1973, both Israel and the Diaspora succumbed to hubris. In the elated aftermath of June 1967, it was presumed that the defeated Arab states of Egypt, Syria and Jordan would come collectively to the negotiating table, as a prelude to regaining their captured territory, subject to border rectifications and the non-negotiable status of reunited Jerusalem. Any suggestion floated in Israel about signing a treaty with Arab states individually, or talking to West Bank Palestinians separately, was vetoed in favour of a comprehensive peace with *all* her neighbours. Now, surely, after such a humiliating defeat, the Arabs would recognise the reality of Israel's existence. Israel only had to sit tight and the Arabs would bow to the inevitable.

The mood in the Diaspora was similarly gung-ho. It was a common occurrence for Jews to be stopped in the streets and congratulated on *their* remarkable victory. Among

American Jews, there were jokes about General Dayan being sent for, in order to sort out the faltering war effort in Vietnam. The American public took to its young ally that had used Western weaponry and technology to crush the Arab clients of Soviet weaponry and technology; a proxy defeat for Communism, to set against the bad news from South-East Asia. President Lyndon Johnson's National Security Council envoy wrote to him that 'after the doubts, confusions and ambiguities of Vietnam, it was deeply moving to see [a] people whose commitment is total and unquestioning'. His preconceptions, which nowadays would be branded as racist, had been overturned. 'Israel at war destroys the prototype of the pale, scrawny Jew; the soldiers I saw were tough, muscular and sunburned. There is also an extraordinary combination of discipline and democracy among officers and enlisted men ...'[1]

It came as an unwelcome jolt when the Arab states, at a summit meeting in Khartoum at the end of August 1967, issued a communiqué of three noes: no peace with Israel, no recognition of Israel and no negotiations with Israel. Major-General Shlomo Gazit, who was in an authoritative position to know, as coordinator of Israeli government operations in the Occupied Territories between 1967 and 1974, makes it clear in his important study *Trapped Fools: Thirty Years of Israeli Policy in the Territories* that the unquestioned assumption was that 'the military occupation would not last more than a few weeks or months, at most'. Such Arab inflexibility had not been anticipated.

The building of settlements in the Occupied Territories began almost by default, an 'if you won't budge, then neither will we' response to Arab obduracy. Retention of the land was an important bargaining chip in any future negotiations. Civilian settlers were allowed on the Golan Heights to tend abandoned Syrian livestock and harvest grain and fruit. But, apart from an intensive building plan for new Jewish neighbourhoods around annexed East Jerusalem, the National Unity government had no settlement policy for the West Bank. Its hand was soon forced.

As early as July 1967, a small group of Israelis, many of them children from four kibbutzim in the Etzion Block halfway between Jerusalem and Hebron that had been captured and demolished by the Arab Legion and local Palestinian militias in the Independence War of 1948, petitioned Defence Minister Dayan to be allowed to resettle there. Dayan refused but they planned to go ahead anyway, announcing a ground-breaking ceremony for September. The problem came to Cabinet, where the minister of agriculture, Haim Gvati, was adamant in his opposition. 'Settlement priorities have to be ... based on security and political considerations and no settlement should be approved just because the government is subject to pressure.' But pressure was precisely what the government *was* subjected to and *ex post facto* approval was given to the Kfar Etzion pioneers. Settler pressure groups soon became the tail wagging the government dog, having quickly identified those Cabinet ministers most sympathetic to their cause.

Yigal Alon, for example, was always regarded by the European Left as a 'good' Israeli, by virtue of his credentials as a secular, socialist kibbutz member. By the same token, he was popular in the Diaspora as a veteran of the elite *Palmach* brigade in the War of Independence, a dashing *Sabra*, along with Moshe Dayan and Yitzchak Rabin, who typified the Zionist 'new Jew'. But his so-called 'Alon Plan', which for many years was the blueprint for any discussion of the future of the Territories, envisaged total annexation to Israel of Gaza and its population, annexation of thirty per cent of the West

Bank with Arab territory in the Jordan Valley surrounded by a tight belt of Israeli settlements and the river Jordan as Israel's political and security border, thus making him a Greater Israel nationalist *avant la parole* and the unlikely ally of ultra-religious zealots. When the firebrand Rabbi Moshe Levinger and his *Gush Emunim* (Bloc of the Faithful) followers occupied a hotel in the centre of Hebron to celebrate the festival of Passover in April 1968 and refused to leave afterwards, in violation of their explicit promise, they had Alon's open support. The government's compromise was to let them build a new settlement, Kiryat Arba, close to the Tomb of the Patriarchs, a site venerated in both Jewish and Muslim tradition. The establishment of an extremist Jewish sect in the middle of a radical Muslim town was a recipe for violence, which culminated in 1994, after a series of escalating incidents, when Baruch Goldstein, a Brooklyn-born settler in Kiryat Arba, went on a murderous rampage while Muslim worshippers were at prayer in the Tomb, killing twenty-nine of them.

On the whole, though, the first ten years of Israeli military rule passed in relative tranquillity. That was due in large part to the 'softly, softly' approach adopted by Moshe Dayan when in administrative charge of the captured territories. His strategy was to maintain a low military profile, to interfere in local affairs as little as possible and to allow an open-bridges policy whereby Arabs in the Territories could resume routine relations with neighbouring countries and visitors from Arab countries could cross the Jordan into the West Bank. It was an imaginative solution to the difficulties of being an occupying power and drew complacent praise from Israeli and Diaspora visitors. 'The most benign occupation in history' was a frequent headline of Israeli PR at home and abroad.

The Israeli public and so-called 'fact-finding missions' from the Diaspora (meaning a quick whirl in an air-conditioned bus to Jericho, the Syrian gun emplacements on the Golan Heights and then a shopping trip to the bazaars of the Old City) were insulated from the realities of life in the Territories by its apparent normality. Between 1967 and 1973, forty-six settlements were built in Judea and Samaria, as it was becoming fashionable to call them after their biblical names, some for military purposes, others by religious militants, without impinging in any obvious way on the Palestinian population. In 1969, in a newspaper interview whose words would come back to haunt her, Prime Minister Golda Meir belligerently denied that there was any such thing as a Palestinian people. The major security problems were elsewhere, either terrorist atrocities against Israeli installations and citizens (for example, plane hijackings, the murder of civilians or the seizure and killing of eleven athletes at the 1972 Munich Olympics) or along the Suez Canal, where a war of attrition was being fought with Egypt, and the Lebanese border, where the PLO (Palestine Liberation Organisation) had installed itself in the south of the country, having been expelled from Jordan after 'Black September' 1970.

Israel and the Diaspora were lulled into a false sense of security. It was disappointing that the Arab states would not respond more positively but Israel had little difficulty in holding on to the Bar-Lev line of fortifications along the Suez Canal and answering every Egyptian provocation with intensive bombardments that reduced Ismailia to a ghost town or cowing Syria with heavy artillery looking down on Damascus from the Golan Heights. From its position of military superiority, Israel could afford to be almost insouciant about the status quo. 'We are waiting for King Hussein to ring us' was Dayan's blithe response to questions about the future of the West Bank, although his, and the Israeli public's, stance on the issue was becoming more complex. The National Religious Party threatened to resign from any government that would give up any part of 'the inheritance of the Patriarchs' for an agreement with Jordan. Even secular Israelis were succumbing to the mystique of place names mentioned in the Bible and insisting that no part of the Holy Land should be declared *Judenrein* (Jew-free). Veteran kibbutzniks fancied that Zionism could rediscover its pioneering imperative in colonising the West Bank. Dayan himself now regarded it as essential to extend Jewish settlement and make it permanent. 'I do think that Israel should stay for ever and ever and ever in the West Bank,' he told a BBC interviewer in May 1973, 'because this is Judea and Samaria. This is our homeland.' He was as forthright in response to foolhardy Egyptian sorties along the canal, declaring that, from Israel's security perspective, Sharm a-Sheikh (overlooking the Gulf of Eilat) without peace was more advantageous than peace without Sharm a-Sheikh.

From a purely military point of view, Dayan was correct. The coordinated attack launched by Egypt and Syria on 6 October 1973, known as the Yom Kippur War by Jews, the Ramadan War by Muslims, caught Israel by surprise and off guard. But the 1967 ceasefire lines gave Israel territorial depth and bought her critical time to mobilise reserve forces and launch a counter-offensive on both fronts. For a few hours, her fate hung in the balance. Over-sanguine intelligence assessments had dismissed the mobilisation of Syrian units and Egyptian army manoeuvres on its side of the Suez Canal merely as exercises to keep the troops in a state of readiness, for defensive purposes, if need be. When 240 Egyptian warplanes flew over the canal to attack Israeli positions in Sinai on the morning of 6 October and 2,000 Egyptian guns opened up an intensive artillery barrage prior to 8,000 Egyptian assault troops crossing the canal, there were just 436 soldiers manning the Israeli fortifications. In the north, where 1,400 Syrian tanks fanned out across the narrow Golan Heights (the same number that the German army had deployed along a 1,000-mile front when it invaded the Soviet Union in June 1941), the Israeli radar and intelligence-gathering centre on the summit of Mt Hermon was defended by one officer and thirteen men.

It took eighteen days of savage fighting before UN Security Council Resolution 338, calling for a ceasefire, was accepted by the three main combatants. On the Golan Heights, the Syrian war dead numbered 3,500 and Israeli dead 722. The Syrians lost 1,150 tanks, the Iraqis more than 100 and the Jordanians 50. Israel lost 100 tanks on the Golan Heights, with a further 250 damaged. On the Suez Canal, Israeli forces had surrounded the Egyptian Third Army that had crossed to the eastern bank, and punched their way to the Ismailia–Cairo road on the western side, as well as cutting the Cairo–Suez road at kilometre 101, leaving Israel in control of 1,000 square miles of additional Egyptian territory. The cost had been high. 1,800 soldiers and pilots had been killed and many more injured. The Israeli death toll on both fronts was just over three times that of the Six Day War.

A pall of gloom settled over Israeli society as the magnitude of the losses was absorbed. In a population of four million, everyone knew someone who had been bereaved or had a tale to tell of smug military ill-preparedness that had required extraordinary examples of heroism and resolve by outgunned and outnumbered units to rectify. The public's anger turned against the government. Prime Minister Golda Meir, Moshe

Dayan, Labour Party veterans and the top echelons of the military bore the brunt of the criticism. The report of the Agranat Commission into the war, partially released within the year, confirmed the public's suspicions of culpability and effectively marked the beginning of the end of the Labour Alignment as the natural party of government.

Less obvious but more profound was the psychological trauma inflicted on Israel and the Diaspora by the war. The sense of Israel's invulnerability had been destroyed. She had only been saved in the early days by large airlifts of American materiel that balanced the vast shipments of the latest equipment, such as surface-to-air missiles and anti-tank weapons, poured into the Arab states from the Soviet Union. When Israel had been on the verge of annihilating the Egyptian Third Army, Secretary of State Kissinger pulled the plug, arranging the ceasefire with Moscow's connivance because he calculated that allowing such a military defeat would be too great a humiliation to permit President Sadat of Egypt to enter into peace negotiations. It was starkly evident that Israel had become militarily, diplomatically and economically dependent on the United States. The Yom Kippur War cost Israel the equivalent of her gross national product for a whole year. Henceforth she had to rely on huge injections of American foreign aid, running at over $3 billion per annum for the past decade. Despite her military flair and capability and technological sophistication, Israel in the modern world was as much the client state of a superpower as ancient Israel had been at the time of the Assyrian, Babylonian and Roman Empires.

The boost to Arab self-confidence was palpable. Israel's image as an invincible superpower had been badly dented. The successful Egyptian crossing of the canal on the first day of the war was an indelible propaganda coup. The oil-producing Arab states, dominated by Saudi Arabia, began to utilise their muscle in the Organisation of Petroleum Exporting Countries (OPEC), embargoing countries that supported Israel and then raising the price of oil to an all-time high. Western economies were under threat. The quid pro quo for stabilising the price of oil was that pressure should be put on Israel in the diplomatic arena. Reflecting the new realities, the song at the top of the pop charts in Israel at the end of 1973 was called 'The Whole World Is Against Us'.

A year later, after the PLO had been legitimised by an Arab summit in Rabat as the 'sole representative' of the Palestinian people, its leader, Yasser Arafat, received a standing ovation at the United Nations. He told the General Assembly, with a pistol in his belt, 'We have entered the world through its widest gate. Now Zionism will get out of this world – and from Palestine in particular – under the blow of the people's struggle.'

On 10 November 1975, by a vote of seventy-five in favour to thirty-five opposed, the General Assembly passed a resolution condemning Zionism as a form of 'racism'. The vote was greeted with defiant anger in Israel and pained disbelief in the Diaspora. Shortly after the Six Day War, Soviet propaganda had started to accuse Israel of using 'Nazi' tactics. Turning a hated epithet against the victims and their descendants was a deeply hurtful and crudely effective propaganda ploy; with time and repetition, the original shock had subsided. Here now was a fresh blow to the collective Jewish psyche. The Zionist vision of rebuilding a Jewish homeland was being lumped in as racist alongside the most detested settler regimes of colonial history.

While Israelis and Diaspora Jews united in mounting a fierce PR international counter-attack, an event took place on the West Bank, little analysed at the time, which was to have an irrevocable effect on the future of the Territories. In December 1975, a persistent group of *Gush Emunim* settlers was given 'temporary' permission by Defence Minister Shimon Peres and Ariel Sharon, intelligence adviser to Prime Minister Rabin, to occupy a former Israeli army camp at Kaddum. Soon afterwards, they pitched their tents on another site, east of Nablus. At the same time, a site four miles east of Jerusalem above the Jerusalem–Dead Sea road, Ma'ale Adumim (Red Heights), was established for strategic purposes.

The floodgates had been opened. Within ten years, there would be 40,000 settlers in dozens of sites throughout the West Bank. The word 'settlement' had a misleadingly cosy ring to it; it suggested rudimentary communities of pioneers, as in cowboy films. In fact, Ma'ale Adumim soon became a major urban centre, an industrial zone linked to Jerusalem by a fast road with a population at the time of writing of over 30,000 residents. It is merely the largest of many such 'settlements', home to more than 200,000 Israelis on Palestinian land.

18 ISRAEL, THE DIASPORA AND LIKUD

In the nine years between the end of the Yom Kippur War and the beginning of the Lebanon War in June 1982, Israel came to depend on Diaspora support for, and interpretation and explanation of, her actions in the Occupied Territories to an increasingly critical outside world. A veteran official of the Anti-Defamation League admitted frankly that by the 1970s American Jewry had become 'an agency of the Israeli government ... following its directions from day to day'.[1] Continued settlement-building and belated international concern over the plight of the Palestinians, who were first uprooted in 1948 and then in 1967 and now living under Israeli military rule in Gaza and the West Bank and expressing their resistance through the PLO, were the subject of constant media reportage.

That the Soviet Union and its Iron Curtain satellites, the Arab states, and the post-colonial countries of the Third World would be hostile to Israel was a given. Harder to accept was the growing coolness in western Europe. Even the USA showed its disapproval on occasion. When Henry Kissinger's shuttle diplomacy between Cairo and Jerusalem failed at first to secure an interim agreement over Sinai in March 1975, President Ford threatened a 'reassessment' of American policy which would have meant, in effect, a suspension of aid to Israel. The threat may have been a spur in Kissinger's second, successful attempt to effect an agreement, signed between Israel and Egypt in Geneva on 4 September. Its additional benefit, from Israel's perspective, was that, in an accompanying memorandum, the United States undertook not to deal with the PLO, as a terrorist organisation that denied Israel's right to exist. But it was hardly coincidental that, at this time of pressure, Jewish lobbying groups in America, searching for the causes of Israel's isolation and falling esteem, decided to embark on an intensive programme of Holocaust education that would result, eventually, in the impressive Washington Holocaust Museum, opened in 1993.

A brief respite from seemingly universal criticism was granted in the summer of 1976, when Israeli commandos staged a spectacular mission to rescue ninety-eight Jewish hostages from a hijacked Air France plane that had been diverted to Entebbe in Uganda after the non-Jewish passengers had been released. In a feat of daring that enthralled the watching world, the volunteer commando unit flew 4,000 kilometres to free the captives, kill their Arab and Ugandan guards and fly them back to Israel unharmed, save for the loss of the unit commander, Yonatan Netanyahu, and one elderly hostage who had been taken to hospital and was murdered there after the raid. Such bravado recalled the heroics of the Six Day War and Israel temporarily basked again in widespread approval. The quotidian problems of administering the

Territories, placating an increasingly confrontational local population and satisfying the demands of the vociferous settler movement were less easily soluble.

When President Carter assumed office in 1977, he soon expressed his intention of taking a more even-handed approach in the Middle East. At a meeting with Prime Minister Rabin in early March, he told him that Israeli settlements on the West Bank were illegal and that the territory under Israeli control would have to be reduced substantially, on the basis of pre-1967 borders. A week later, in a speech in Massachusetts, the president said that 'there has to be a homeland provided for the Palestinian refugees who have suffered for many, many years'.

One constant feature of Labour-led coalition governments in the decade after the Six Day War, whatever their changing personnel, was firm opposition to the idea of a third, Palestinian state between the Mediterranean and the Jordan. Ministers maintained discreet contact with King Hussein in the hope of reaching an understanding with him about the future disposition of the West Bank ('the Hashemite option'), thereby sidestepping Palestinian nationalism. But the canny ruler, whose precarious kingdom depended on financial subsidies from other Arab states and whose population was sixty-five per cent truculent Palestinian refugees, was not inclined to step out of Arab line in order to risk his life on a separate peace agreement with Israel.

The sense of drift and contradiction at the heart of government policy-making was plain to see. In contrast to Labour uncertainty, the Likud opposition, an alignment of right-wing parties, promised a clear alternative for the future of the West Bank. Faithful to Jabotinsky's dream of a Jewish state on both sides of the Jordan, his loyal Revisionist follower, Menachem Begin, would incorporate Judea and Samaria into a Greater Israel that offered to its Arab residents limited municipal autonomy under Israeli jurisdiction. Likud's manifesto for the general election of May 1977 called for acceleration in the 'setting up of defensive and permanent settlements, rural and urban, on the soil of the homeland' – meaning all of the West Bank.

In addition to this radical contrast of policy, Likud was untainted by fallout from the errors of the Yom Kippur War. There was a public perception that Labour had failed to address the mistakes of that war, was the party of privilege, had not reformed corrupt institutions and had grown complacent from uninterrupted tenure in office. A risible no-confidence vote, prompted by the delivery of the first batch of new F-15 fighter jets from the USA too close to the commencement of Sabbath, led to the removal from government of the National Religious Party, which had been a necessary prop of all Labour-led coalitions since 1948. Stung by its loss of Cabinet portfolios and political patronage, the NRP threw in its lot with the opposition. Following financial scandals, both the minister of housing and a prominent figure in the Labour establishment committed suicide. Finally, Rabin himself was forced to resign in April 1997 after news broke that he and his wife had failed to close a small but illegal bank account that they had held from their time in Washington when he had been the Israeli ambassador. Rabin's constant and distrusted rival, Shimon Peres, became acting prime minister just three weeks before the election.

Nevertheless, the result of the vote was the greatest political shock in the state's, and before that the *Yishuv*'s, history. Labour won only thirty-two seats, its worst-ever result, while Likud emerged as the largest single party with forty-three seats, its best-ever result. That Begin, the former terrorist leader of the outlawed Irgun group, should now be the democratically elected premier of Israel was greeted with dismay in the Diaspora. He had what pollsters would call an 'image problem', not least in the UK, where his part in blowing up the British army's headquarters at the King David Hotel in Jerusalem, with the loss of nearly one hundred lives, had not been forgotten.

The PR agencies, lobbying committees and fund-raisers rose to the challenge, most of all in the USA, where widespread ignorance of Zionist history was matched by facile acceptance of the 'Holocaust = suffering, Israel = redemption' nexus, one which Begin, a Polish-born escapee and superb orator, could skilfully exploit in order to silence critics of his hardline policies. American Jewry's most prominent spokesman, Rabbi Alexander Schindler, chairman of the Conference of Presidents of Major American Jewish Organisations (a clumsy title for the committee that brings together the foremost movers and shakers in American Jewry), was frank about his major aim: to make Begin acceptable not only among Jews but, more importantly, in the White House.

It was a difficult task in a predominantly liberal Diaspora, which overwhelmingly supported every 'territorial compromise' plan for the future of the Territories over annexationist schemes. Only a tiny, mainly religious, right-wing minority approved the accelerating settlement drive. One of the first things Begin had done on assuming office was to introduce officially into the geographical lexicon the biblical names of Judea and Samaria; he refused to use any other term. But uneasy Diaspora Jews were lulled when, in November 1977, President Sadat made his historic visit to Israel and addressed the Knesset (Parliament). Ezer Weizman, who was the

Israeli minister of defence, hospitalised as the result of a car crash and watching on television, expressed the feelings of most Jews when he wrote: 'Our enemy set foot on Israeli soil. The unbelievable was happening.'

Ten months later, on 17 September 1978, the Camp David Accords were signed by President Carter, President Sadat and Prime Minister Begin. There were two accords. The first outlined an autonomy plan for Gaza and the West Bank, to be followed after five years by a permanent settlement that would recognise 'the legitimate rights of the Palestinian people and their just requirements'. The second laid down the framework for concluding a peace treaty between Israel and Egypt. At last, after thirty years, it would be possible for Israelis to cross one neighbouring border. In their jubilation, many Jews were willing to suspend judgement on Begin and hope that the leopard was capable of changing its spots.

Begin submitted the Camp David Accords for Knesset approval. In doing so, he risked rejection from Likud extremists, who were opposed to autonomy for West Bank Palestinians and withdrawal from all of Sinai, where eleven settlements were home to nearly three thousand Jews. But he correctly banked on support from the other parties and secured a comfortable majority, by eighty-four votes to nineteen, with seventeen abstentions, among them Yitzhak Shamir, his eventual successor as prime minister. On 26 March 1979, the peace treaty with Egypt was signed in Washington. Returning Sinai, which had no historical resonance in Jewish folk memory, was a price that Begin was ready to pay in order to prise Egypt from the Arab coalition and leave himself free to interpret West Bank 'autonomy' as he chose. In December he travelled to Oslo to receive the Nobel Peace Prize.

During 1980 he oversaw the largest expansion yet of settlements in Gaza and the West Bank – thirty-eight of them, mostly in heavily populated Arab areas, joined the forty-nine that had been built over the previous three years.

There could be no doubt of his intention to establish a permanent Jewish presence throughout the Occupied Territories, sealing their attachment to Israel. Despite mounting concerns about continued military rule that was having a corrosive effect on the morale of the army and infringing Palestinian civil rights, Diaspora leaders still dutifully parroted the official line emanating from Jerusalem. They told Jewish doubters that any criticism should be expressed privately; to do so publicly would be 'giving comfort to Israel's enemies'. Keen pupils of their hero Jabotinsky's dismissive epithets for his political opponents but lacking his propensity for elegant invective, Likud supporters labelled those who broke solidarity with Israel as 'traitors', 'Arab lovers' or 'self-hating Jews'. Non-Jewish criticism was 'anti-Semitism masquerading as anti-Zionism'.

The tenor of government pronouncements became more strident, a blend of paranoia (tiny Israel against the world), vigorous self-justification and manipulation of the Holocaust to justify Draconian collective punishments in response to terrorist attacks and civil disobedience in the Territories. Operating under British emergency measures from 1946 that had never been rescinded, the military authorities employed preventive detention, expulsion, book censorship, the blowing up of the houses of suspected terrorists, the closure of schools and universities and curtailment of legal redress, all in the vain attempt to quell unrest. Prime Minister Begin's speeches and interviews deflected censure by brooding obsessively on past Jewish persecutions and their lessons for modern Israel.

When West German Chancellor Helmut Schmidt spoke of the rights of Palestinians, Begin retorted that Schmidt, a young *Wehrmacht* officer in the Second World War, 'had remained faithful to Hitler until the last moment'. Survivors accused him of demeaning the memory of the Holocaust, but Begin was accurately gauging the mood of large segments of Israeli society, for whom frustration at worsening terrorism, economic privation and a self-absorbed Labour Party too busy picking over the wounds of electoral defeat to offer a coherent alternative had hardened into an ugly xenophobia. Picking up on the mood, Begin's new defence minister, Ariel Sharon, warned that the Arabs of Greater Israel should 'not forget the lessons of 1948'. Annexation of the West Bank and the Golan Heights was openly called for, with the solution of 'population transfer' to their 'natural homeland' in Jordan (hence the 'Jordan is Palestine' slogan) for those Palestinians who would not accept Israeli citizenship.

In January 1981, Begin announced that new elections would be held in six months' time. Shortly before Israel went to the polls, he ordered an air force unit to bomb a nuclear reactor being built in Iraq with uranium supplied by France. The raid was successful and hugely popular, despite Shimon Peres' wan complaint that it was an election ploy. If so, it succeeded. Begin was re-elected, with an additional four seats. As previously, his most enthusiastic support came from voters of 'the Second Israel' (unskilled workers, the low-waged, disaffected Sephardim resentful of years of Labour's paternalistic indifference, taxi drivers, recent Russian immigrants, small business owners) who hailed him at his rallies as 'Begin, king of Israel' and blatantly intimidated opposition meetings.

Once more, loyal Diaspora organisations obediently fell into line. Their standard response to numerous and more public Jewish critics of Israeli foreign policy was that their function was to support the people and democratically elected government of Israel, irrespective of which political party was in power. An added riposte, much favoured by Nobel Prize winner Elie Wiesel, was that only those who lived there had a right to criticise Israel, although he frequently ignored his own admonition when speaking out from New York against abuses in the Soviet Union and other countries.

But it was becoming harder to hold the line. During 1982 the government announced plans to increase the settler population to 100,000 by the end of the century (in actuality, it was more than double that by the year 2000) and allocated £33 million for thirty new settlements, part-civilian, part-military, to be built that year. In Israel itself, public protests increased. In May, six senior reserve officers called a press conference at which they testified about 'atrocities' committed by Israeli soldiers as a consequence of the 'repressive measures' in force on the West Bank. They blamed Defence Minister Sharon for 'corrupting' young conscripts by ordering them to provoke clashes with unarmed civilians. 'The daily reality in the Territories is one of violence and brutality ... We are gradually losing our humanity. The local population are gradually becoming objects in our eyes – at best mere objects, at worst something to be degraded and humiliated.' They cited the case of an Israeli soldier who had written the identity numbers of detainees on their forearms, doing so by grim coincidence on Holocaust Remembrance Day.

Concerns about the corrupting effect of occupation on the morality of the soldiers enforcing it were not new. In 1969 a noted Orthodox scholar, Yeshayahu Leibowitz, who was virtually unique among those of his religious outlook in denouncing the golden calf of worshipping territory, had written: 'I do not worry about what the occupation will do to the Palestinians; they have already survived many occupations. I worry about what it will do to us.' But it was unprecedented for serving officers to speak out in protest. More than 80,000 demonstrators marched in Tel Aviv against Sharon's 'iron fist' policy.

On 3 June 1982, an assassination attempt on the Israeli ambassador in London left him totally paralysed. The gunman belonged to a small, dissident group fiercely opposed to Arafat's leadership of the PLO. On 6 June, Israeli troops crossed the Lebanese border and advanced northward in an attack codenamed 'Operation Peace in Galilee'. Its stated aim was to establish 25-mile cordon sanitaire in order to end repeated incursions and rocket attacks against the towns and kibbutzim of Upper Galilee from the PLO bases in southern Lebanon. Sharon assured an emergency Cabinet meeting that the campaign would be localised and take only two or three days to flush out the PLO. On that basis the militarily inexperienced Cabinet gave its assent, as did the opposition parties. It was the justification peddled by government spokes-men and dutifully recycled by Israel's Diaspora apologists.

But when the limited 'Operation Peace in Galilee' turned into 'Operation Big Pines' – an ambitious scheme hatched by Sharon and his chief of staff to destroy the PLO militarily, install Bashir Jemayel, the Christian Phalangist leader, as Lebanese president and through him to conclude a second Arab peace treaty with Israel – the consensus within Israel, and between Israel and the Diaspora, broke down irretrievably.

19 THE SEA CHANGE

The Lebanon War of 1982 marked a watershed in Israel–Diaspora relations. They have never been the same since. It is hard to recall, at this distance of time, the excessive respect that Diaspora communities used to accord to Israel's representatives. From ambassadors to humble press attachés, their English might have been less than perfect, their manners a little uncouth when contrasted with the suave envoys of other countries, but that was part of their rough-hewn integrity, their 'difference'.

No doubt, in the Israeli version of Diplomatic Charm School, Likud appointees were given lessons on how to deal with the anxieties surfacing in a less than complaisant Diaspora that until 1977 had only been used to conducting relations with Labour-led governments. Self-important communal big-wigs would be summoned to a briefing by the ambassador, or one of his underlings, who would begin by quoting, to polite laughter, Sir Henry Wotton's remark that an ambassador is an honest man sent abroad to lie for his country, but that was not their way. They would admit that, yes, Israel was facing problems, grave problems. Here the speaker would lean forward, take the listeners into his trust, caution secrecy and then give them some piece of banal information about Syrian armaments or Iraq's nuclear potential that could have been gleaned from a casual reading of the previous week's newspapers. The communal bigwigs, privy to momentous secrets, would file out and duly tell rapt audiences how, only the other day, the ambassador had told them, in confidence... And the embassy could report back that the Jews in that country were holding firm with Israel.

All that changed with the Lebanon War. Unquestioning acceptance is no longer given to the words of visiting politicians from Jerusalem and, although 'the centrality of Israel in Jewish life' is still the catchphrase trotted out by fund-raisers and educationalists in the USA and other major centres of Diaspora Jewish domicile, contributions to Israel have fallen off over the past two decades as greater financial support is being paid instead to local communal institutions.

Some of the schemes dreamt up to counter this trend and bolster closer identification with Israel, especially among the young, have been tacky in the extreme. During the 1990s, for example, before the second *intifada* (Palestinian uprising) put paid to it, there was the 'March of the Living', in which thousands of Jewish adolescents from around the world, mainly American, toured the concentration camps in Poland, where they commemorated Holocaust Remembrance Day before flying to Israel to celebrate Independence Day. This Holocaust to Redemption tour hammered home the Zionist message. At Auschwitz, a rabbi informed participants that the world divided neatly into two parts – those who had actively aided the Nazis and those who had passively collaborated with them. At Maidanek, another rabbi told them that the camp could become operational again within a few hours. Israeli security guards accompanying the tours accentuated the sense of hostility and danger by constantly warning the youngsters to stop for nothing and run straight for the buses in the event of an incident. Another scheme on similar lines was a simulated trip of Jewish DPs (displaced persons) to Haifa, replicating the ill-fated voyage of the *Exodus* in 1947 when the ship was seized by the British and the refugees on board forcibly returned to Hamburg. A caustic Israeli commentator suggested that they weren't utilising their tragic potential to the full – at Masada, Israel could develop a theme park with 'Romans', 'Zealots' and a mass suicide to save parents the price of a return ticket for their offspring![1]

Israel's misconceived foray into Lebanon in June 1982, which was sold to the Cabinet, the Israeli public and the Diaspora on the basis of a false prospectus, had dramatically visible and immediate consequences; the creeping erosion for many Jews of their faith in Zionism would emerge later. The brutal bombing of refugee camps, the towns of Tyre and Sidon, and Beirut while under three-month siege; the choice of a brilliant brigade commander to resign rather than lead his tank column in the assault on Beirut's Muslim western sector, with inevitable civilian casualties; and, above all, the massacre in Sabra and Chatila refugee camps of 2,300 Palestinian men, women and children by Christian Phalangists while Israeli forces sealed off the camps – all of this convulsed Israeli public opinion, divided the Diaspora vehemently and shocked the world, watching the daily images of Israeli destruction on TV. A mass rally in Tel Aviv of 400,000 protesters, more than ten per cent of the population and the largest explosion of public outrage in Israel's history, demanded a judicial commission of inquiry into the Sabra and Chatila massacres. The government was forced to bow to public pressure.

The resultant Kahan Report was uncompromising in its conclusions. It censured the chief of staff, the director of military intelligence and officers in the army's Northern Territorial command, criticised the prime minister, concluded that the minister of defence had not fulfilled his duty and called on him to 'draw personal conclusions'. Sharon declined to do so but was forced out after the Cabinet voted to adopt the report's recommendations, though he remained as minister without portfolio. He was made of more obdurate fibre than his prime minister. Seriously affecting Begin's health and judgement were the daily protests outside his home, the mounting military losses and the patent evidence that Israel, by choice, had started a war that was sucking her ever deeper into the Lebanese quagmire. During the siege of Beirut, his jubilant remarks about having trapped Hitler in his bunker already gave cause for concern, while, equally surreal, Arafat–Hitler skipped through the rubble demanding to know who the real terrorists were now. He obdurately refused to give in to the demand that he recognise the existence of Israel, even though it was undoubtedly Israeli bombs and artillery raining down on him. A reclusive Begin, mourning the death of his beloved wife, resigned in 1983. It would be another seventeen years and many more deaths before the last Israeli soldiers were finally withdrawn from southern Lebanon.

The consequences of Begin's and Sharon's disastrous attempt to impose a *Pax Hebraica* on the region and root out Palestinian nationalism have been analysed exhaustively elsewhere. For the purposes of this book's argument, it only needs to be reiterated that the Lebanon War was the cause of a sea change in the Israel–Diaspora relationship, as surely as there was a causal link between Israel's prolonged involvement in Lebanon and the first *intifada,* which broke out in Gaza and the West Bank six years later. In the Diaspora, as in the Occupied Territories, people detected signs that Israel, for all her military potency, had badly misjudged the situation. Having itemised the hundreds of dead soldiers and thousands wounded, and the alarming rift that the war had opened up in Israeli society, Israel's most respected military analyst, the journalist Ze'ev Schiff, wrote in 1985, 'one may be forced to conclude that a country can be victorious on the battlefield but lose a war strategically; that a small nation whose leaders fail to appreciate the limits of military power is doomed to pay dearly for their arrogance...'[2]

One instance of the Diaspora's new-found readiness to stand up to Israel concerned Jewish emigrants from the Soviet Union and their ultimate destination. The number of exit permits granted to Jews had steadily increased from the mid-1980s, due in the main to American–Soviet agreements which specifically linked trade with the granting of exit visas. As had been the case for over a century, most Russian Jews yearned to go to the *goldeneh medina* (America), but for an equally long time Zionists had regarded the Russian–Jewish masses as the most likely population reservoir for rebuilding the homeland. A state that had been founded on mainly Russian labour and was ninety-five per cent Ashkenazi when established in 1948 now had a sixty–forty ratio in favour of Eastern Jews. Culturally, educationally and ethnically, Russian Jews were desirable immigrants if not tempted elsewhere. 8,155 permits were issued in 1987 but only 2,072 of the recipients went to Israel. By 1989, exit visas had risen to an unprecedented 71,000, but only 12,117 of that number ended up in Israel.

A passionate debate ensued, with the Israeli government insisting that every Russian emigrant with an Israeli visa in his passport should be obliged to go there, while the American–Jewish aid committees argued that every departing Russian Jew should be allowed freedom of choice. In the end, it was a policy decision of the United States government, arrived at for economic reasons, which prevailed. A quota system was imposed, limiting Russian–Jewish immigrants to the USA to 50,000 a year. All other Soviet applicants would have to go elsewhere. Israel was the beneficiary by default. 185,000 Russian Jews arrived in 1990 and almost as many the following year. Housing and absorbing them was a vast task, undertaken with a verve and improvisation that caused resentment among Sephardic immigrant communities, who felt that favouritism was being shown to Ashkenazim in order to redress the demographic balance. In insisting on the right of Russian Jews to live where they chose, the Diaspora establishment publicly demurred from following Israel's wishes in a way that would have been unthinkable before the failed Lebanon adventure.

Equally significant were the number of support groups set up in America and Europe to publicise Israeli organisations such as Peace Now, *Yesh G'vul*, a body of reserve soldiers opposed to service beyond the Green Line, or *B'tselem*, a civil rights group that monitored abuses in the Territories and soon established itself among foreign journalists and media as a reliable, objective source of information. Diaspora Jews penned articles in newspapers and journals disassociating themselves from the actions of the Likud government, something else that was rare before Lebanon.[3] In the correspondence columns of Jewish newspapers, dissenting letters began to appear more frequently, counterbalancing the standard justifications for Israeli policy.

These were still minority symptoms, but, where previously those few in the Diaspora who criticised Israel could be lumped together as disaffected lefties, embittered place-seekers or self-hating Jews, now eminent academics and well-known public figures were adding their voices to a growing chorus of unease. Representative bodies deplored this 'washing of dirty linen in public', which, of course, simply exacerbated it, as did some of the bizarre arguments put forward in defence of the Lebanon War. In America, for example, Norman Podhoretz, editor of the widely read magazine *Commentary* and fresh from having rewritten the Vietnam War as a noble venture undermined by weak politicians, coyly put himself on a par with Zola by writing a piece after the Sabra and Chatila massacres entitled *J'accuse* which charged anyone who dared utter a word of criticism against Israel of being *ipso facto* an anti-Semite. He followed up in 1985 with an even more egregious piece of nonsense that 'proved', contrary to popular perception, that Israel had been the winner in Lebanon. In the UK, Melvin Lasky, editor of the CIA-funded *Encounter* magazine, was another last-ditch, retrospective defender of the war.

The stock-in-trade counter to those who presumed to pass moral judgement on the Lebanon debacle or Israel's retention of the Territories was to summon up memories of the Holocaust and to level the charge of having double standards. No other countries had the right to criticise Israel after their guilt by commission or omission during the Second World War. Anyone who asked Israel, which was insistent on being the only democracy in the Middle East, to behave as befitted

Judaism's traditional teachings and *better* than, say, Syria or Iraq was guilty of hypocrisy and demanding of the Jews standards which they did not apply to others.

In Israel, the election of July 1984 reduced Likud's number of seats to forty-one, but, habitually distrustful of Shimon Peres, the voters only increased the Labour Alignment's share to forty-four, not enough to form a viable coalition. The extraordinary spectacle ensued of a National Unity government in which Peres and Shamir rotated the premiership, each serving for two years at a time. This recipe for foreign policy inertia at least slowed the pace of settlement on the West Bank and enabled the economy to be brought under control after a period of four hundred per cent per annum galloping inflation.

In 1988, Palestinian frustration at the hardships of military rule erupted in a movement of resistance throughout Gaza and the West Bank. The *intifada* bore all the hallmarks of the spontaneous national uprising that Ben-Gurion had identified and warned about in the Arab Revolt of 1936 to 1939. It was Shamir's turn as prime minister when the *intifada* broke out. His inflexible response, implemented by Yitzhak Rabin as defence minister, and the army's inability to quell stone-throwing mobs other than by the use of disproportionate force, ensured widespread support for the resistance among the inhabitants of the Territories. The PLO leadership was forced to watch impotently from exile in Tunis, whence it had been banished with 10,000 fighters after the siege of Beirut.

The situation worsened over the following three years. In September 1991, the Israeli army issued figures of known deaths since the uprising had begun. 1,225 Arabs had been killed, 697 (of whom 78 were aged fourteen or younger) by Israeli soldiers and the remaining 528 in Arab-on-Arab killings for alleged 'collaboration with the authorities'. Thirteen Israeli soldiers had been killed and nearly 100 civilians in knifings and suicide attacks. In addition, more than 2,000 Palestinian houses had been seized or demolished, 120,000 trees uprooted in reprisal actions and on any given day 14,000 Palestinians (one per cent of the population) were held in preventive custody. According to *B'tselem*, as many as 4,500 Arabs had been tortured while under detention.

Less tangible but equally significant results of the *intifada* were the strangulation of the Palestinian economy, with 140,000 workers deprived of their employment in the Israeli labour force, and the coarsening effect on soldiers forced to undertake policing duties. A military court, while sentencing four Israeli soldiers accused of torturing and killing Palestinians, wrote in its verdict: 'We were amazed to hear from several of the witnesses expressions of hatred and contempt for human life regarding the Palestinian population under our military rule … We believe the four defendants were not an exceptional case and were no different from thousands of other soldiers …'

Following the swift annihilation of Saddam Hussein's army in the Gulf War of 1991, in which Arafat foolishly supported the Iraqi dictator while Israel acquiesced reluctantly to American pleas for restraint, and the disintegration of the Soviet Union at the end of the year, leaving the USA the world's sole superpower, the international climate was propitious for a fresh initiative to try and solve the Israeli–Palestinian crisis. Despite Prime Minister Shamir's wonted negativity and refusal to negotiate directly with the PLO, a conference was convened in Madrid under the joint sponsorship of Presidents Bush and Gorbachev, followed by further talks in Washington. Shamir, dragged unwillingly to the table, further exasperated the Americans by asking for $10 billion in loan guarantees towards the absorption of new Russian immigrants, without halting building activity on the West Bank. His days, however, were numbered.

In the Israeli general election of June 1992, the hegemony of Likud, which had ruled almost unbroken since 1977, was ended. Labour, now led by Rabin, who had recently ousted his perennial rival Peres as party leader, won a convincing victory and was able to form a coalition government, to the barely concealed satisfaction of Washington and the bulk of Diaspora Jewry. A simple test of the Diaspora's relationship with Israel is that it always feels happier with a Labour-led government, which at least *talks* about territorial compromise, than with a Likud government wedded to its vision of a Greater Israel.

To almost universal surprise, Rabin, the hardline soldier whose notorious recipe for quelling the *intifada* had been to 'break the bones' of rioters, now displayed statesmanlike qualities in the search for a solution. Aided by Peres, the practical but flexible technocrat, as foreign secretary, Rabin told the Knesset that his government would quest for peace with 'fresh momentum', determined to turn 'a new page in the annals of the State of Israel'.

Rabin was true to his words. Despite a worsening situation on the ground with daily battles in the streets and intensified killings, talks began in strictest secrecy with the PLO. Successive Israeli governments had refused to deal with the PLO and Shamir had sacked Ezer Weizman from his Cabinet for meeting with Arafat in Vienna, but the PLO appeared as a force for restraint and moderation compared to Hamas and Islamic Jihad, the two Muslim fundamentalist groups most opposed to any compromise with Israel and both growing in popularity among the young of Gaza and the West Bank as a result. Through the good offices of the Norwegian government, a series of meetings was held in Oslo between Israeli and Palestinian negotiators between January and March 1993.

At an official level, the post-Madrid talks dragged on inconclusively in Washington. In Gaza, the West Bank and Jerusalem, the number of murdered Israeli soldiers and civilians continued to rise, as did the severity of the military response. In Oslo, however, the secret talks were progressing well. Senior government officials joined the Israeli delegation, reflecting the seriousness of the discussions. Finally, on 20 August 1993, the negotiators initialled a document, the Oslo Accords. Almost a month later, on 13 September, Yitzhak Rabin and Yasser Arafat signed the Declaration of Principles on the White House lawn and exchanged a reluctant handshake.

It really did seem, at last, after the wars and cruel deaths of innocent men, women and children on both sides, that Israel would now be accepted and live in peace with her Arab neighbours. The Diaspora shared in the general euphoria. But hopes quickly faded in the harsh environment of the Middle East.

20 FROM OPTIMISM TO DISILLUSIONMENT

Once begun with that handshake on the White House lawn, the peace process appeared to gather its own momentum. The Oslo Declaration of Principles was greeted with enthusiasm in the Diaspora and warmly approved of in Israeli and Palestinian opinion polls but extremists on both sides tried to sabotage progress. Islamic Jihad and Hamas, dead set against recognition of, or peace with, 'the Zionist entity', turned to a new terror tactic – the suicide bomber. For their part, Israeli settlers were adamantly opposed to any withdrawal from the West Bank sites which were sanctified in their eyes by mention in the Bible.

Rabin and Peres pushed on determinedly with the transferance of swathes of Gaza and the West Bank to Palestinian control. Consciously echoing Ben-Gurion's remark at the beginning of the Second World War about fighting Hitler despite the White Paper, Rabin declared that '[w]e will continue the [peace] process as if there is no terror. And we will fight terror as if there is no process.' After months of negotiation which were stalled by Baruch Goldstein's massacre of twenty-nine Muslim worshippers in a Hebron mosque and two equally shocking revenge attacks by Hamas suicide bombers, an agreement was finally signed in Cairo on 4 May 1994 (President Mubarak's sixty-sixth birthday), whereby Palestinian self-rule was granted to all of Gaza and an area around Jericho. Arafat thereupon discarded his title of chairman of the Palestinian Authority for the more imposing designation of president, a would-be head of state. A peace treaty with Jordan soon followed, signed by Rabin and King Hussein in Akaba on 26 October, in the presence of President Clinton.

Three days after the Jordan signing, 2,500 Israeli, Arab, American and European politicians and business leaders met in Casablanca at an economic summit hosted by the Moroccan king. It was signalled as the start of closer cooperation throughout the region, particularly between Israel and the Arab states, with the aim of bringing prosperity to all their peoples in a Middle Eastern version of the Marshall Plan.

Buoyed by these positive signs, Yossi Beilin, Israel's deputy foreign minister and one of the architects of the Oslo Accords, gave way to hubris in a number of contentious articles which were published in the Diaspora and forecast that, by the year 2025, the American Jewish community would have dwindled to no more than one million, European Jewry would have all but disappeared and the vast majority of the world's fourteen million Jews would be living in the State of Israel.

At the time, there was superficial plausibility to his scenario. Highly qualified immigrants from the former Soviet Union were still entering Israel in their thousands. The economy was booming in the new spirit of hope and optimism engendered by peace treaties with Egypt and now Jordan, progressing self-government for the Palestinian inhabitants of Gaza and the West Bank and the start of negotiations with Israel's most intractable neighbour, Syria. Buildings were going up as exuberantly as in reunified Berlin, superhighways were being constructed which, it was said, would one day link Jerusalem to Cairo and Damascus, high-tech industries were transforming the coastal plain into a miniature Silicon Valley and Shimon Peres' vision of a Middle Eastern Common Market, galvanised by Israeli drive and know-how, seemed closer to realisation.

It was Mark Twain who attributed to Benjamin Disraeli the aphorism that 'There are three kinds of lies: lies, damned lies and statistics'. One could add a fourth lie – 'demographic projections'. Graphs never behave with remorseless exponential logic, no matter how painstakingly statisticians compile them. The rosy future that Beilin painted for his country depended crucially on a satisfactory solution to the Israeli–Palestinian conflict; without it, all his demographic projections were built on quicksand.

So it has proved. The spate of terrorist attacks and suicide bombings intensified, with the Palestinian Authority unable or unwilling to root out the instigators in Gaza and the West Bank. For his part, Rabin was too weak politically, in public opinion, in the Knesset, where his majority depended upon two Arab seats, and even in his own party, to openly confront the settler movement and curtail its activities. Even when the Israeli army had withdrawn from Gaza, sixteen settlements remained in the heart of the Strip, an inevitable focus of confrontation with the local Arab population and the Palestinian security forces. Likewise, the Israeli government demurred from removing the fifty heavily guarded Jewish families living in the centre of Hebron, despite the simmering animus of local residents after Baruch Goldstein's killing spree.

Worsening terrorist outrages made Israeli public opinion increasingly apprehensive about handing over more of the West Bank to Palestinian autonomy, but negotiations pressed ahead to conclude Phase II of the Oslo Accords. A complex plan had been devised for the staged withdrawal of the Israeli army from areas incrementally ceded to the Palestinian Authority. Oslo II was signed in Washington by Rabin and Arafat on 28 September 1995.

'Traitor' was the epithet most frequently hurled at Rabin by right-wing demonstrators, religious fundamentalists and settler groups. In the Knesset, he was accused by an opposition politician of leading 'an insane government that has decided to commit national suicide'. At one protest, an empty coffin with Rabin's name on its side was paraded. At another, leaflets were distributed with a caricature of Rabin in the uniform of an SS officer. Rabin's foremost political opponents – Ariel Sharon, the rising Likud demagogue Binyamin Netanyahu and Rafael Eitan, chief of staff during the Lebanon War – so incited a rally in Jerusalem that the crowd called for the deaths of the 'Oslo criminals' Rabin and Peres.

The mood in Israel was more polarised, ugly and emotionally violent than at any time since the issue of German reparations divided the nation in 1953. At a mass rally in support of Oslo II on the evening of 4 November, Rabin, usually shy and retiring to the point of brusqueness, spoke as a military man, with fervour and conviction about his desire for peace. His oration included the words: 'Violence erodes the basis of Israeli democracy. It must be condemned and isolated.'

A few minutes later, Rabin left the platform and was fatally shot by Yigal Amir, a 23-year-old religious student whose spiritual leaders regarded any withdrawal from biblical land as a betrayal of eternal Jewish values.

Rabin's assassination stunned Israel and appalled the Diaspora, where religious and secular opponents of the Oslo Accords had also given vent to intemperate invective. But, shocking though political assassination is to Western sensibilities, it is by no means unique in Zionist history. In 1983, at a Peace Now demonstration against the Lebanon War, Emil Grunzweig, a 33-year-old paratroop officer who had fought in Lebanon, was killed by a grenade thrown into the crowd. In 1933, Chaim Arlosoroff, the highly regarded political secretary of the Jewish Agency and *bête noire* of the Revisionists, was shot dead by two assailants while strolling along the Tel Aviv beach with his wife. The biblical description by the spies sent out by Moses of 'a land that eats up its inhabitants' (Numbers XIII, 32) still has chilling contemporary resonance.

Shimon Peres, a man whose appetite for power is only exceeded by his inability to utilise or retain it once it is in his grasp, took over as prime minister. The obvious *tactical* thing to have done would have been to call an election shortly, when he could have counted on a clear mandate from sympathetic voters. Like Lyndon Johnson with civil rights legislation after the assassination of President Kennedy, he could then have pressed ahead with more daring initiatives than would have been otherwise possible. Instead, he chose to continue trying to implement Phase II of the Oslo Accords, despite terrorist attacks of greater carnage, ruthlessness and frequency than anything yet experienced. A despairing population was increasingly drawn towards Likud's denunciations of the peace process and calls for 'peace with security', a shorthand phrase for abandoning the Oslo Accords.

Faced with bitter internal divisions, eroding support in opinion polls and a timetable for phased West Bank withdrawal that was in tatters, Peres bowed to the inevitable and called a general election for May 1996. To compound the shambles, on the eve of the election and to convince voters that he was tough on terrorism, Peres launched 'Operation Grapes of Wrath' in response to shelling by Hezbollah ('Party of God', an Iranian-trained terrorist group) from across the Lebanese border. It went horribly wrong. In the village of Cana, 105 Lebanese civilians were killed by incorrectly calibrated Israeli artillery. Strong international condemnation and US mediation forced Israel to end the bombardment of fundamentalist strongholds. Opposition parties seized on the propaganda bonus, accusing the government of having caved in to outside pressure and thereby giving the green light to terrorism.

After a campaign that was even more rabble-rousing, febrile and intimidatory than those that had brought Begin to power, the result of the election was that Binyamin Netanyahu won a slim majority of the popular vote for prime minister, although the Labour Party emerged with the largest single number of Knesset seats – thirty-four against Likud's thirty-two. Netanyahu was able to form a coalition with the nineteen seats of the religious parties, seven seats of a new and right-wing Russian immigrant party led by Natan Sharansky and four members of the centrist Third Way Party.

Once again, an Israeli election result posed a dilemma for the Diaspora. The secular, liberal values of Labour-led coalitions sat more easily with Diaspora Jews than the strident slogans of Greater Israel nationalists, hardline Russian immigrants and ultra-Orthodox zealots. On the other hand, Netanyahu was a glib communicator, who had learnt his presentation techniques on the American political circuit. He was persuasive on television. Ostensibly committing himself to upholding the Oslo Accords and participating in talks with the Palestinians under American sponsorship, in reality Netanyahu obstructed further implementation by delaying the withdrawal from Hebron and rural areas, as agreed in Oslo II, blaming the Palestinian Authority's failure to curb terrorism in the vicinities already under its control.

Mutual distrust intensified after Netanyahu unilaterally gave permission for opening an ancient tunnel that ran under the Old City, adjacent to the Temple Mount; its exit was in the Muslim quarter, but Palestinians feared that the status of the holy places was being jeopardised. In the ensuing violence, fifteen Israeli soldiers and fifty-six Palestinian civilians lost their lives.

The sharp divisions within Israeli society – between left and right, rejectionists and accomodationists, religious and secular, Ashkenazi and Sephardi – also intensified. The government was mired in a political scandal, with charges of malpractice reaching up to the prime minister himself. It was claimed that a clandestine deal had been struck between the Attorney-General and one of the religious parties whereby the Shas ('Sephardi Torah Guardians') leader, Arye Deri, would be protected from a corruption indictment in return for delivering crucial votes on a parliamentary motion. Netanyahu defended himself by vigorously attacking left-wing politicians and media commentators who could not, he asserted, accept that he was the electorate's choice.

A decision to build homes for as many as 32,000 Jews on Har Homa, a hillside on the southernmost boundaries of post-1967 Jerusalem, was a clear signal that Oslo was being discarded, despite a United Nations vote of 130–2 (the USA and the Pacific island group of Micronesia) condemning the proposed construction. An increasing number of Palestinian homes in East Jerusalem were razed to the ground, allegedly because the occupants had not obtained the requisite building permits. It was, in fact, part of a deliberate attempt to reduce the Palestinian population of Jerusalem by refusing to renew identity cards and giving those without them fifteen days' notice to leave. A flurry of building on the West Bank, with settlements designated as 'national priority areas' and residents tempted to move there by low mortgages and other inducements, left no doubt about Likud's ultimate intentions. Unveiling the so-called Bailey Plan in the summer of 1997 simply confirmed them. According to the plan, the Palestinians would receive three or four enclaves, totalling forty per cent of the West Bank and ruled by the Palestinian Authority, while Israel would retain the rest of the land under her sovereignty, including the principal water aquifers, tracts of territory along the West Bank's borders with Israel and a corridor from Jerusalem to the river Jordan that would cut the area in half.

In blithely announcing that the plan was something he had 'offered', Netanyahu neglected to mention that he had not bothered to discuss it beforehand with the Palestinians. It provoked the most serious, sustained impasse in Israeli–Palestinian talks since the mutual recognition of 1993. Inevitably, violence followed. On 30 July 1997, two suicide bombers blew themselves up in Jerusalem's main market, killing sixteen shoppers. The government responded by suspending the movement of Palestinian workers into Israel and freezing financial transfers to the Palestinian Authority, thereby cutting off sixty per cent of its funding. Further terror attacks ensued. As the mother of a 14-year-old schoolgirl killed by a suicide bomber said: 'When you put people under a border closure, when you humiliate, starve and suppress them, when you raze their villages and demolish their houses, when they grow up in garbage and in holding pens, this is what happens.'

Israeli society was riven, although, having to brace itself against the most sustained criticism of Israel since the Lebanon War, the Diaspora, was, by contrast, enjoying a period of tranquil affluence in the United States and unexpected regeneration in Europe. The collapse of Communism had loosened the restraints that had previously kept eastern Europeans circumspect about admitting that they came from Jewish ancestry. Having a Jewish genealogical strand became almost a chic fashion accessory among young, newly emancipated Europeans. As they migrated westwards in search of job opportunities, eastern European Jews reinvigorated moribund communities. Germany had the fastest-growing Jewish population in Europe, boosted by 60,000 Russian immigrants. Holland's 30,000-strong Jewish community was augmented by an estimated 10,000 expatriate Israelis, with a similar phenomenon evident in New York, Los Angeles, London – any centre of Jewish population where, simply put, it was safer to walk the streets than in Jerusalem or Tel Aviv.

Ironically, it was the Wye River Memorandum of 23 October 1998, transferring additional areas to Palestinian control and negotiated by Netanyahu in order to mollify the Americans, which would be the cause of his downfall. Angered by his concessions, the maximalist right abandoned Likud to form the National Unity Party. Coalition anarchy, worsening security and the breakdown of any relationship with Arafat and the Palestinian Authority left Netanyahu no option but to call a general election for May 1999.

The convincing victor was Ehud Barak, the recently chosen leader of the Labour Party, who had campaigned under a slogan promising to continue the Rabin legacy. A former chief of staff and conservative by instinct, Barak had been opposed to the Oslo Accords, a fact that he and the media conveniently overlooked when he presumed to don the mantle of the fallen leader. He had trodden the well-worn path in Israel from army to politics, which to the perplexity of outsiders bears little correlation between personal ideology and choice of party but simply depends upon where greater preferment lies.

Despite widespread relief at the political demise of Netanyahu and high hopes for a better accord with the Palestinians, Barak offered little improvement. He constructed his coalition with a bias towards right-wing and religious parties. During his brief tenure, settlement-building actually increased by ten per cent. Insofar as Barak had a strategy, it appeared to be trying to reach an agreement with Syria in order to marginalise the Palestinians. As he said, 'Achieving peace with Syria would greatly limit the Palestinians' ability to widen the conflict.' He failed in that, and when, belatedly, he and his negotiating team met face to face with Arafat and his advisers at Camp David for two weeks in July 2000, with President Clinton mediating, those summit talks too ended in failure.

Depending upon which narrative you read, blame for the failure of one of the most exhaustively analysed summits in diplomatic history either lies with the Palestinians in general and Arafat in particular (according to the American and Israeli version as set forth by Dennis Ross, President Clinton's special envoy to the Middle East, and Shlomo Ben Ami, Barak's chief negotiator) or with the American and Israeli teams (according to the version of, among others, Robert Malley, Clinton's special assistant for Arab–Israeli affairs).

What becomes apparent from the welter of blame-apportioning is that the summit was badly mishandled on a tactical level, a realisation retrospectively acknowledged by all three sides. The Palestinians were reluctant participants, feeling that they had been 'bounced' into it by American and Israeli pressure. They suspected America's ability to act as an impartial mediator. The chemistry between Barak and Arafat was dismal – the Palestinian president was sulky and characteristically ambivalent while the Israeli prime minister exhibited the compensatory cockiness of many small men and behaved like an arrogant customer beating down a bazaar salesman in the Old City. Neither side had a clear perception of its end goals. According to one report, the Palestinian delegation did not even arrive with its final-status maps. President Clinton, keen to end his term of office with a historical triumph, pushed too hard.

The immediate result of the Camp David failure was an escalation of Palestinian terrorism and the evaporation of popular support among Israelis and Palestinians for the efficacy of continued negotiation. In a symbolic gesture that wrote *finis* to the process begun in Oslo seven years previously, Ariel Sharon made a highly publicised and heavily guarded visit to the Temple Mount, near the al-Aqsa mosque, Islam's third holiest shrine. It triggered a predictable outburst of Palestinian violence and the inevitable military response. Apologists for the robustly secular Sharon claimed that he was merely asserting the right of Jews to pray at the site of the destroyed Temple, but Jabotinsky's heirs appreciated, as their mentor had, a gesture's potency. The 1929 Arab riots had followed Revisionist insistence on praying at the Western Wall.

The first *intifada* had been a spontaneous popular uprising of stone-throwing and civil disobedience; the second, given the religiously charged title of the *al-Aqsa intifada*, quickly developed into an armed revolt. Even so, the initial Israeli reaction was sanguine. I happened to be in Israel at the time and recall reading an article in *Ha-Aretz* newspaper by Ze'ev Schiff in which he wrote that Israel could cope indefinitely with such low-level violence – more people were killed weekly on the roads. A series of suicide bombings soon put paid to such a complacent analysis. According to an

Israeli security service report issued at the end of 2002, the Palestinians had sent out 145 suicide bombers during the first two years of the *al-Aqsa intifada*, forty of whom were identified as being affiliated with Fatah, fifty-two with Hamas and thirty-five belonging to Islamic Jihad; eighteen were individual acts.

Those who suspected that Arafat had been waiting for a pretext under which to unleash terror were confirmed in their suspicions. A more objective assessment is that Arafat and the Palestinian Authority were not strong enough to control events. The *al-Aqsa intifada* was a revolt not only against repressive Israeli occupation but also against a Palestinian leadership that was deemed internally corrupt and too submissive to Israel. Suicide bombers, in contrast, were lauded as supreme martyrs to the Palestinian cause. Never a decisive leader, Arafat was in a quandary. To take on the Islamic fundamentalists would have precipitated a Palestinian civil war; not to condemn terrorist outrages would have invited harsher Israeli retaliation.

Arafat's declining prestige among his own people and Barak's plummeting support among Israeli voters prompted two further attempts to reach an agreement, in December 2000 and, finally, in February 2001 at the Egyptian resort of Taba. The negotiators at Taba came tantalisingly close to resolving the issues that had divided them at Camp David but by now it was too late. Barak was a lame-duck premier, with all the opinion polls forecasting that he would be trounced in the forthcoming general election and Sharon announcing that he would not be bound by any agreement signed by his predecessor. The *intifada* had gathered its own momentum which Arafat was powerless to restrain, even had he wanted to.

Ariel Sharon was duly elected prime minister in March 2001. The voters were willing to overlook his dubious past record for expectations of the strongman who would deal with terrorism and restore a semblance of normalcy. In airbrushing his portrait for national and international consumption, the image-makers made much of the assertion that Sharon's thinking had evolved. He was no longer the maverick general or devious architect of the Lebanon War but recognised the painful adjustments it would be necessary for Israel to make. After all, it was he who had supervised the evacuation of the Sinai settlements when in Begin's government. Thus did hope spring eternal among Israel's well-wishers about Revisionist leopards changing their spots.

Certainly, Sharon's first move domestically demonstrated statesmanlike wisdom – or a shrewd calculation of the opposition's venality. Although comfortably able to manage with a purely right-wing coalition, he invited the defeated Labour Party to join a government of National Unity. Benjamin Ben Eliezer, the party chairman who for a time had served in the army as Sharon's subordinate, found the offer of the defence portfolio too tempting to resist. He was joined, inevitably, by the perennial place-seeker Shimon Peres, who justified his defection with the ludicrous excuse that his presence in the Cabinet would restrain Sharon and ensure a continuation of the Oslo process.

The Palestinian situation remained in stasis, with the continuing cycle of terrorist attacks and tough Israeli retaliations. Having already sanctioned a policy of 'targeted assassinations' against those deemed responsible for master-minding Palestinian terrorism and armed resistance, the Twin Towers outrage of September 2001 afforded Sharon the opportunity to ally Israel with President Bush's War against

Terror. Israeli spokeman bracketed Arafat with Osama bin Laden, and a suicide bombing which killed twenty-nine celebrants and wounded 150 at a Passover *Seder* meal in the coastal resort of Netanya on 27 March 2002 furnished the provocation to take action. Two days later, Israel launched 'Operation Defensive Shield'. Tanks and infantry units, supported by Apache helicopters, rolled into Palestinian Authority areas of the West Bank and Gaza.

With its goal of wiping out the Palestinian terror network, the invasion was systematic, comprehensive and destructive. 8,500 Palestinian suspects were arrested, and a civilian infrastructure of radio and television stations, databases, power plants, water treatment facilities and roads was put out of commission. Resistance, especially in the refugee camp of Jenin, was answered with overwhelming firepower. Because Israel closed off media and rescue access to the area, lurid and grossly exaggerated rumours of massacre and wanton destruction circulated, drawing widespread criticism and condemnation.

Two events that did receive intense media scrutiny were the siege of the Church of the Nativity in Bethlehem, in which a group of Palestinian militiamen had sought sanctuary, and the encirclement of Arafat and a core of his officials in his headquarters (the *Muqata*) in Ramallah. It required the pope's personal intervention to lift the church siege and American mediation to secure Arafat's survival. International preoccupation with these two events meant that an unprecedented Saudi-sponsored proposal put forward at a summit conference of Arab States in Beirut – for peace with Israel in exchange for a withdrawal to her pre-1967 borders, the establishment of a Palestinian state and a just solution to the refugee problem – passed virtually without analysis or exploration.

An ageing Sharon's antipathy for a fragile Arafat, which predated their confrontation during the siege of Beirut, mirrored the growing alienation between two peoples whose only unnatural contact was in circumstances of oppressor and oppressed, terror victim and terror perpetrator. Less than ten years after Oslo had been greeted with optimism by the majority of Israelis and Palestinians, each's dehumanisation of the other was commonplace. An Amnesty International report of October 2002 listed 250 Palestinian and 72 Israeli children killed until that month since the second *intifada* began. According to Israeli figures, 625 Israelis had been killed in terrorist attacks and 4,500 injured, with 1,372 Palestinians killed by Israeli military forces. The Palestinian Red Crescent dubiously calculated over 20,000 Palestinians injured over the same period.

The situation was bleaker than ever and Sharon had not proved to be the desired saviour. At the end of October 2002, the National Unity government collapsed when Labour voted against the proposed budget, ostensibly because it allocated too much money to settlement at the expense of welfare and internal development. Nevertheless, in the January 2003 general election, Sharon easily defeated Amram Mitzna, the leader of a demoralised Labour Party since Barak quit politics to become a commentator and talk-show 'expert' on Arab affairs in the build-up to the American-led invasion of Iraq.

Since then, Sharon has talked frequently of his readiness to negotiate about the contours of a Palestinian state once its leadership halts terrorism. President Bush has also uttered the statehood word, provided that the Palestinian Authority reforms its institutions, renounces terror and embraces his favourite concept of democracy. A new American initiative, the so-called 'Road Map', has replaced the discarded Oslo Accords. A security fence – in some places a wall – continues to be built by Israel along the West Bank, as a physical deterrent to terrorist incursions and suicide bombers. Yasser Arafat has died in Paris and perennially hopeful analysts saw it as a fresh opportunity for a new Palestinian leader to emerge with the incompatible assets of both acceptability to Israel and authority among his own, increasingly radicalised, constituency, enabling him to enter into fruitful negotiations. All this, plus Sharon's decision to withdraw unilaterally from Gaza, outraged the religious and nationalist parties, which left his coalition. But 81-year-old Shimon Peres once again answered the call of duty, this time giving as his reason for entering the National Unity government of 76-year-old Ariel Sharon that it would help speed the Gaza withdrawal and induce Likud to vacate more of the West Bank than the few isolated settlements so far on offer. In the event, the evacuation of Gaza passed off virtually without incident, despite alarmist prognoses.

In 1948, the British Labour politician Richard Crossman, a keen supporter of Israel in the days when she had many admirers on the left, described the new state as a young democracy ruled by a gerontocracy. Ben-Gurion was a mere stripling of sixty-two at the time.

As for the Diaspora, it looks on with increased scepticism, mounting embarrassment at trying to defend nearly four decades of Jewish colonisation of another people's land and weary despair at every fresh revelation of army brutality towards Palestinian civilians. Stale arguments by Israel's most fervent supporters, including American Evangelical Christians, about Arab intransigence, about a fundamentalist jihad bent on destroying Israel and supported by all Arabs, wear thin when confronted by images of the occupation.

The validating myth of the Israeli military used to be 'purity of arms'; that it waged war only in self-defence, with restraint and magnanimity towards the enemy. Nowadays, such a principle would be greeted with derision by the soldiers themselves. Enforcing rule over two million resentful inhabitants of the West Bank, subjecting them to roadblocks and identity checks that can make the twenty-kilometre journey from Jericho to Jerusalem a five-hour odyssey, arresting them arbitrarily in terrorist swoops, demolishing houses and olive groves as collective punishment while fearful all the while of booby traps and ambush or that the veiled woman approaching along the road might be carrying a bomb under her robes have corroded their humane instincts, soured their better feelings and tarnished their youth.

It is not without political advantage to those engaged in the thankless task of furbishing Israel's image whenever an anti-Semitic incident in Europe – vandalising a Jewish cemetery, daubing graffiti on a synagogue, setting fire to a community centre – occurs. The spectre of anti-Semitism as the longest hatred can be utilised to persuade Jews to stifle their concerns, close ranks and reaffirm their solidarity with Israel. Even so, one sustaining fallacy of two thousand years of Diaspora survival, the sense of being specially chosen and morally superior, has been shattered for ever by Israeli history since 1967. When faced with testing circumstances and forced to decide between the categorical imperatives of Kantian ethics or conforming to group self-interest, one has seen that Jews respond no differently from and no more or less admirably than any other religious or ethnic collectivity of human beings.

21 TAKING STOCK; ISRAEL AND THE DIASPORA TODAY

If this book has taken up a disproportionate amount of space in sketching Israel's political and strategic fluctuations since the Lebanon War of 1982, it is because Israel takes up a disproportionate amount of time in the thinking and concerns of Diaspora Jews. It could be said that 'the Israeli problem' has replaced 'the Jewish problem' as a neurosis in search of a cure.

According to the most recent statistics, 5,260,000 Jews live within Israel proper, alongside 1,350,000 Arab citizens. In addition, in Gaza and the West Bank are a further 3,800,000 Palestinian Arabs. Although accurate figures are harder to come by, it can safely be calculated that nearly twice as many Jews, some 9,500,000, live in the Diaspora. The combined Jewish communities of the United States and Canada comprise nearly fifty per cent of that total and almost all of the remainder live in the world's most advanced, industrialised countries, where civic equality for all citizens is the norm. Despite the warning in the previous chapter against overreliance on demographic projections, it is an unavoidable conclusion that, unless the Diaspora immigrates en masse to Israel – something that Western, acculturated Jewries have been notoriously reluctant to do – within twenty years there will be more Palestinians than Jews living between the Mediterranean and the river Jordan given their respective birth rates of 1.2 per cent among Jews against 3.1 per cent for Arabs. A geographer at Haifa University has calculated that, by the year 2020, a total of 15,100,000 people will live in the territory of historic Palestine, with Jews comprising a minority of 6,500,000.[1]

Naturally, Israeli think-tanks, long-range strategists and sophisticated media analysts are well aware of the political implications of these statistics. They are engaged in a vigorous debate. Where they differ and argue most vociferously is in how to respond to a disturbing scenario. It is a modern-day replay of the dilemma that has perplexed the Jewish state since biblical times – how does a relatively small entity maintain itself among covetous and more numerous neighbours? The differing responses are categorised in contemporary parlance as hawks against doves or neocons against liberals. Because there is little new under the sun, the author would propose that what we are seeing, yet again, is that perennial Jewish debate between accomodationists and absolutists; between those who would settle for half a loaf rather than risk losing the whole bread; between those who opt for the Diaspora way of adaptation and compromise and those who stick to the rigid Zionist formula of never apologising and never explaining; finally, between those who would prefer to choose life as a canny dog who is able to learn new tricks and those who prefer to choose death as a brave but obdurate lion.

Demographic facts suggest to the pragmatist that there is an urgent need for Israel, if she wishes to remain a Jewish state, to reach a broadly acceptable accommodation about the future disposition of Gaza and the West Bank that enables her to live in security and acceptance among her neighbours, before she is overwhelmed by their numerical superiority. The only alternative offered by the absolutist is to take permanent refuge behind an 'iron wall' that pens Israelis in while keeping enemies out and to depend for ultimate survival on a client relationship with the United States that remains improbably stable in perpetuity, unlike the usual shifts and transitions in strategic alliances between sovereign states. If all else fails, the last resort would be to remember Masada and unleash nuclear weapons – hardly a counsel of optimism to set before one's citizens.

Israel has yet to demonstrate, after more than five decades of statehood, that she is capable of pursuing the accomodationist course. Her acceptance in the family of nations is still disturbingly provisional. The occasional correspondence column musings, usually by elderly officers who served in the Mandate's Arab Legion, about whether it was such a good thing after all to vote in 1947 for the creation of Israel can be dismissed as merely eccentric; nobody suggests that Zimbabwe, North Korea or other 'rogue states' should be disestablished just because we dislike their leaders' policies. But the regular flotation in academic circles of the bi-national state concept for solving the Israel–Palestine conflict is a more significant and worrying marker for those who wish to retain Israel's role as *the* state of the Jews. The partial success of 'cold' peace treaties with Egypt and Jordan has to be set against the unremitting, sapping expenditure of human and material resources in regular large-scale wars and smaller campaigns. Terrorist atrocities are an existential fact of life for Israelis. It was Herzl's hope that Zionism would break the mould of insecure Jewish existence in the Diaspora and enable Jews to 'live as free men on their own soil, to die peacefully in their own homes'. For Jews, that is more likely to happen almost anywhere in the world than in Israel.

One of the ways that Zionism, in its infancy, chose to present itself to European sympathisers was as an outpost of western civilisation in the backward Orient. Although the make-up of Israeli society is now as Eastern as it is Western, that image, with its colonial resonances, still prevails and has been sharpened by the so-called 'clash of civilisations' between the values of Western-style global capitalism and reactionary Islamic fundamentalism. Culturally and legislatively, Israeli civic society is founded on Enlightenment principles that reach back to the American and French Revolutions. Those are the principles that President Bush and his neo-conservative advisers are currently seeking to impose on Iraq, the Palestinian Authority and elsewhere in the Middle East. In countries based on tribal and religious loyalties, resistance to the Western values that Israel has espoused serves to accentuate her interloper status in the region.

In itself, that does not automatically preclude her integration. After all, the history of the Middle East from biblical times onwards furnishes numerous examples of different societies, cultures and religions finding a modus vivendi and cross-fertilising. Pessimists would argue that such harmony rarely lasts and the weaker eventually succumb to the stronger, but nation states, like peoples, come and go. When Israel was voted into existence in 1947, there were fifty-six members of the United Nations. Today there are more than three times that number.

Unfortunately, the patiently acquired Diaspora skills of compromise, conciliation and adjustment – in diplomatic parlance, Henry Kissinger's doctrine of 'constructive ambiguity' whereby negotiating parties agree to some general principles that each can wishfully interpret as its own triumph and implement accordingly – did not percolate down to those who staff Israel's strategic think-tanks and foreign ministry. Such skills were not only mislaid, they were positively rejected when the Zionist pioneers arrived in Palestine. For their offspring, the *Sabra* generations born in the *Yishuv*, honest talking (i.e. telling the truth without diplomatic niceties) was a sign of fearlessness, the antithesis of Diaspora humility before a gentile lord or master. The word for it in *Sabra* slang was *dugri*, with connotations of no frills, simplicity and directness; it was borrowed from Arabic, in which it means 'straight'. Regrettable though it may be, the language of diplomacy is 'straight' only when the strong are laying down the law to the weak; otherwise, it depends on nuance, accompanying gesture, the suggestion of unspoken possibilities, all of which the French-schooled Arab elites are adept at and plain-speaking Israelis are not.

A newcomer visiting Israel is impressed by the bustle and vitality and cowed by the aggressive rudeness. It must be the worst-mannered society in the world. In contrast to an average Israeli, a New York cabbie appears to have all the polish of a courtier at Louis XIV's Versailles. There are extenuating reasons, of course. Israel is a nation constantly fearing bad news, avidly listening to the hourly bulletins, always edgy and insecure. Its society is more pressure cooker than melting pot, as every variety of Jew from Russian blond to Ethiopian black, from ultra-Orthodox *Chasid* to pig-eating secularist, noisily jostles for recognition and special treatment.

Such a volatile environment is not conducive to the leisurely rhythms of polite social intercourse, nor does it encourage the cultivation of diplomatic skills. Any Diaspora Jew who has sat in on exploratory dialogues between Israeli and Palestinian representatives is struck by the urbane veneer of the Arab participants and the relative gaucherie of the Israelis. Their ill-concealed impatience with a recitation of Palestinian grievances and brusque dismissal of them with the stock response, 'Yes, yes, both our peoples have suffered [although what Palestinians have inflicted on Israelis is hardly symmetrical with what the might of Israel has visited upon the Palestinians] but now we must move on' reveals an absence of the empathy essential if two hostile peoples are ever to be reconciled.

It was ever so. Dealing with the Arabs came low on the list of pre-state priorities. At the time of the serious Arab riots of 1929, after forty years of colonising in Palestine, there was no Arab department and few Arab-speakers in the Jewish Agency nor was any Arab-language newspaper published by the Zionists. Even today, the most dovish of Israeli politicians, those most willing to make far-reaching concessions, can display unconscious condescension in their dealings with Palestinians. Their fluent but harshly accented English (a speech trait shared by many settler societies) puts one uncomfortably in mind of Afrikaner farmers talking about their natives.

It is pertinent that Israel's most effective diplomat, Abba Eban, was more popular abroad than at home. Domestically, his orotund Hebrew speeches bemused listeners, whereas his sonorous orations in English received rapt attention at the UN and were acclaimed by Diaspora audiences. South-African-born and Oxford-educated, Eban was of the right age, in the right time and place, to play a significant role in the early days of statehood. Thereafter he was shunted aside to play ambassador to the gentiles, the acceptable face of Israeli foreign policy on the international stage but adrift and with no power base in the tight, inward-looking world of party politics. In that respect, if no other, he resembled Jabotinsky, whose cosmopolitanism made him suspect in the eyes of his narrowly focused contemporaries.

Modern Diaspora Jews, almost by definition, are universalists, familiar with wider culture. They have a composite identity, made up partly of their Jewish heritage and partly of the history, literature, language and sense of unique national character of the polity in which they are citizens. They are American Jews, English Jews, French Jews and so on, as there are American Catholics, English Catholics and French Catholics, the adjective being of at least equal weight to the noun in all countries where there is a separation of religion and state under the jurisdiction of civil law. At the height of the siege of Beirut, a powerful American Jew met with Prime Minister Begin to tell him how harmful Israel's invasion was to Jewish interests. Heated words were exchanged. As Begin showed him the door, he said to his visitor: 'You have to choose between being a Jew or being an American.' Diaspora history has been one long exercise in successfully evading that choice and the accompanying accusation of dual loyalties.

Modern Israeli Jews, on the other hand, especially if born there, have a discrete ethnic identity. They have no enriching or conflicting – depending on your point of view – accretions of external culture. They may have acquired through education, but have not absorbed as components of their identity, both Jewish sources alongside Melville and the Civil War if American Jews, Magna Carta and Shakespeare if English

Jews or Voltaire and the Rights of Man if French Jews – or Goethe and *Bildung*, as German Jews did. Almost by definition, Israeli Jews are ethnocentric, particularist and dismissive of the Diaspora legacy as shameful, less worthy. The Zionist assumption of being the 'real' Jews, of inherent superiority to anything on offer in the Diaspora, can have amusing manifestations. I recall on my first visit to Israel in 1957 being offered tomatoes at supper by the mother of a kibbutz friend. 'Do you have tomatoes in England?' she inquired. When I answered that, yes, we did, she was temporarily stilled but then responded brightly, 'Ah, but not as big as *our* tomatoes!'

Sense of humour is a revealing signifier in the context of cultural differences between Israel and the Diaspora. Israelis are hardly renowned for their humour, not only because life is too stressful, but also because the Jewish sense of humour is quintessentially a product of Diaspora experience. Two jokes, of many, illustrate the point.

The first concerns two Jews about to be shot by a tsarist firing squad. The officer in charge asks if they have any last requests. One says that he would like a handkerchief to cover his eyes. His friend nudges him and murmurs, 'Yankel, don't make trouble.'

The second is about the Galician immigrant who goes to a Savile Row tailor and asks him, in broken English, to make him a gentleman's three-piece suit. The suit fits perfectly. He then asks for a bowler hat. That too fits perfectly. He completes the outfit with a rolled umbrella. The tailor assures him that the entire ensemble looks superb but is disconcerted to see that his customer is crying and asks why. Answers the Jew: 'I'm crying for our lost empire.'

Both those jokes are born of a deprecatory self-awareness of Diaspora survival stratagems; to keep a low profile and remind the parvenu not to imagine that he can hide his Jewishness by becoming more Catholic than the pope. The Zionist would retort that precisely *that* is the Diaspora problem; only in Israel can Jews lead a full, unself-conscious life without fear of anti-Semitism. The irony is that, if there has been a renewal of anti-Semitism in countries such as France, with its large Muslim population, it is because of controversial events in the Middle East involving Israel. The Jew in the Diaspora is caught up willy-nilly in Israel's treatment of the Palestinians and assumed guilty by association.

Most Diaspora Jews are willing to accept that bearing the brunt of anti-Israel criticism is the price they pay for supporting the right of a Jewish state to exist within secure, internationally recognised borders. Jewish nationalism is no less defensible than any other recognisable national movement, possibly more so, given the circumstances in which the State of Israel came into being. But, sixty years after the Holocaust, Israel can no longer claim 'special case' status to justify repression of Palestinian national aspirations or 'historical right' (whatever that means) to defend retention of biblical territory captured in war. It affronts Jews, with their memories of persecution, when phrases such as 'settler regime' or 'Bantustan policies' are used to describe Israel's administration of the Territories. Israel is a democracy, her supporters never tire of pointing out, the only one in the Middle East. But, since 1967, she has been a *Herrenvolk* democracy (the term coined to describe South Africa under apartheid), in which one group of subjects, the Israeli citizens, enjoys full rights while a disenfranchised group, the Palestinians, enjoys none of any significance.[2]

It is in the field of civil rights that Diaspora support for Israel is stretched most tautly. One of the reasons for choosing to remain in the Diaspora, rather than responding to the

Zionist challenge, is the civil liberty Jews take for granted in all free societies. Equality under the law is the cornerstone of democracy. When that principle is not applied to 3,800,000 Arabs under Israeli occupation, the Diaspora Jew is hard put to defend the abuse and deprivation of Palestinian rights when Israeli settlers, living illegally on their land, enjoy the full protection of Israeli law. Over a century ago, on a visit to Palestine, Achad Ha-Am, Zionism's most enduring writer, was so distressed at how badly the Jewish settlers behaved towards the indigenous population, 'infringing Arab boundaries, resorting to violence and treating their neighbours with contempt', that he feared the outcome, should Jews ever become the majority in the land, and concluded with the Talmudic plaint 'let the Messiah come and let me not [live to] see it'.[3] The realisation of one's hopes sometimes turns out to be more tangled and painful than the failure to realise them.

Israel's immediate and short-term prospects are not encouraging. Whichever Palestinian leadership emerges in the post-Arafat era, the starting point for Palestinian negotiators whenever talks resume will be what was so nearly achieved at Taba in 2001 with regard to the return of most of the West Bank, the final status of Jerusalem and a mutually acceptable resolution of the refugee problem. A Likud-led government will insist on negotiating from its own, less forthcoming blueprint. Meanwhile, waiting in the wings to obstruct progress and capitalise on any impasse will be the radical Islamic factions bent on Israel's destruction and the Greater Israel fundamentalists determined to stay in their settlements, come what may. Israel's population is pessimistic, low on morale and deeply divided. Sober analysts debate the possibility of civil war should settlements in Judea and Samaria be dismantled as were those in Gaza; settler groups had already warned

Sharon that he would suffer Rabin's fate if a West Bank pull-out occurs. In November 2005, frustrated by the intransigence of right-wing supporters, Sharon left the Likud party, to form his own, more centrist one. He was joined, of course, by Shimon Peres. Two politicians with a combined age of 160 years uniting under the banner of a party called 'Forward' suggests that Israelis might have a sense of humour, after all. Since Sharon's grave stroke, opinion polls predict yet another coalition government. By its very nature, the most that a National Unity government can achieve is to put a brake on extremist excesses, but otherwise it is designed to hamstring all but the most cautious initiatives. The despair and sense of drift, except among those with their own baneful agenda, calls to mind the lines of W. B. Yeats: 'The best lack all conviction, while the worst / Are full of passionate intensity.'

The Diaspora, by contrast, is flourishing. Statisticians and the religiously Orthodox point out an elderly average age, birth rates below the national averages in the West and intermarriage running at around fifty per cent in America and Europe. In common with most mainstream religious denominations in the West, organised worship is in decline. Few Jews attend services on a regular basis and the ancient tenets of the faith, from not eating forbidden food to 'marrying out', are observed only by the tiny Orthodox minority who warn apocalyptically that assimilation will complete the work of Hitler. But their definition of Jewish status is the increasingly inoperable one of having a Jewish mother or having converted to Judaism under the auspices of a recognised (i.e. Orthodox) Rabbinic Board. In Israel too, where the overwhelmingly secular majority have their personal status determined by Orthodox criteria, it is no longer possible to hold the traditional line. At a conservative estimate, 250,000 of the Russian immigrants over the last two decades do not conform to the *halachic* (religious law) definition of being Jewish. One of the reasons why non-Orthodox Judaism, which ninety per cent of synagogue-affiliated Jews in America belong to, is growing steadily in Israel and elsewhere in the Diaspora is because it makes conversion to Judaism easier and has a welcoming approach to mixed-faith couples and their children.

Religious practice may be waning in the Diaspora but ethnicity is in vogue, from wearing knitted skullcaps to playing *klezmer* music at weddings. Jewish cultural activity is lively and varied. In contemporary society, where religion is a matter of personal profession, the Diaspora Jew picks and chooses what to practise. As belief has lost its hold, Jews have found compensation in 'tradition', meaning a nostalgic fondness for the customs of their forebears, whether in studying Yiddish or dancing the *hora*. In the fluid world of mass communication, global markets and multinational corporations, Jewish personnel move around the big cities, meet partners of different nationalities and faiths and, if so inclined, make contact with the local community. Expatriate Jews are a standard component of synagogue membership in Europe's major commercial centres. They turn up in less likely places, too. In Cuzco, on the Inca Trail, there is a Jewish delicatessen, run by Israelis. Nowadays, there are as many Israelis in New York and Los Angeles as in Tel Aviv.

Such mobility and ease of movement was unimaginable in the heyday of the nation state, when Zionism first conceived the notion of transplanting the downtrodden Jewish masses of the Russian Empire to a rebuilt homeland in Palestine. Migration is the standard response to social and economic pressures, which is why there are now sizeable Filipino and Turkish diasporas in the labour force of every European and Asian city and workers from eastern Europe are doing the menial jobs in affluent economies. In Israel, as waiters in cafés and on building sites, Romanians and Ukrainians have replaced the Palestinians barred since the *intifada*.

As always throughout history, Diaspora Jews are adapting to novel circumstances and responding to changing times. Two thousand years of powerlessness have honed their antennae to detect where self-interest lies, what is or is not attainable and how far to adjust in order to persevere. The experience acquired over two and a half millennia of learning to live circumspectly among more numerous and powerful neighbours is a surer guarantee of survival than the triumphalist illusions of a mere fifty-odd years of statehood. In 1967, with stunning victory in the Six Day War, the Zionist construct of the new, different, independent and powerful Jew reached its apotheosis. But, as Israel has discovered since, power brings its own constraints, no less than powerlessness. As she has tried to cope with the problems of ruling over a resentful, dispossessed people, the contrast between those Jewish qualities nurtured by two thousand years of marginalised Diaspora existence without a homeland and the grubby realities of maintaining an embattled Jewish state has become starker. Certainly, what Israel's constant inability to come to terms with the limitations of military power when dealing with her neighbours does demonstrate is that the historic Diaspora techniques of adjustment, flexibility, wariness and accommodation were not such contemptible stratagems, after all.

The State of Israel could learn much from a proper application of the lessons of Diaspora history. In the words of the Talmudic homily with which we began, 'It is better to be a live dog than a dead lion.' But that is not in the nature of the 'new' Jew constructed by the early Zionists in conscious reaction to the contingencies of Diaspora existence.

22 'THE FOX KNOWS MANY THINGS, BUT THE HEDGEHOG KNOWS ONE BIG THING'

In the years after the Lebanon War of 1982, the Israeli ambassador in London was a passionate orator who liked to work a favourite anecdote into his speeches. 'For a time,' he would say, 'and unbeknown to each other, Theodor Herzl and Sigmund Freud lived on the same street in Vienna. Imagine what would have happened if one day Herzl had knocked on Freud's door and said: "Doktor, I have had a dream"?' Having captured his listeners' attention with such a novel possibility, the ambassador would then paint a vivid picture of how the dream had been turned into reality, list Israel's many achievements and assure audiences that even greater triumphs lay ahead if only peace could be concluded with the Arabs.

In the London district of Hampstead, where every third resident is a Jewish psychoanalyst, so the joke goes, there is a Freud Museum. The museum opened a new wing in memory of Freud's daughter Anna and invited the Israeli ambassador to be the guest speaker. Clearly, he had no more idea of what he was doing there than his audience had of why he had been invited, but he launched into his standard anecdote as being vaguely appropriate. When he delivered its punchline about imagining what might have had happened if Herzl had said to Freud, 'Doktor, I have had a dream', from the back of the hall someone muttered, *sotto voce,* 'Perhaps he would have cured him!'

The suppressed laughter with which a largely Jewish audience greeted that remark, out of respect to the guest speaker, was symptomatic of growing Diaspora unease, then still confined to a minority, at the path Israel was taking. It was an apt setting in which to express anxiety. Herzl's dream about establishing a Jewish homeland and his mental condition at the time have been fruitful seams to mine for psychoanalysts, historians and biographers alike. According to his diary, he was in a frenzy of fevered excitement while writing *The Jewish State*, his only relaxation being evenings at the Paris Opera listening to the exalted strains of Wagner's *Tannhäuser*. There is another apocryphal and chronologically impossible anecdote which posits Hitler at the same production on the same night as Herzl. Its punchline is that Wagner's music inspired the one to write *Der Judenstaat* and the other *Mein Kampf*.

Fanciful though the Herzl–Freud, Herzl–Hitler stories are, since Hitler would have been a precocious 8-year-old at the time, what is the reason, as the rabbis of the Talmud would begin their legal questioning, behind them? What allegorical lessons are they designed to convey?

In the case of Herzl–Hitler (with the notoriously anti-Semitic Wagner as an added bonus), the message is fairly clear. Herzl's way led to redemption through Zionism, Hitler's to the culmination of centuries of persecution in the Holocaust, aided and abetted by the siren calls of gentile culture. Improbably linking the Zionist Messiah with the arch-Satan illustrates the enduring impact of anti-Semitism on the Jewish collective psyche and why it is still virtually impossible to discuss Zionism rationally and unemotionally. Such is the ethos of the state, and so has it been inculcated into generations of her citizens and their Diaspora supporters that, in the last resort, Israel's justification will always be anti-Semitism, and the memory of the Holocaust will always be invoked to place her outside the usual canons by which political behaviour is judged. Anyone wishing to make a critical comment about Israel is obliged to preface it with acknowledgement of Hitler's unparalleled barbarism; any reference to Palestinian displacement and suffering is countered with a litany of longer and greater Jewish suffering; any observation about terrorism being the inevitable reaction of people living under indefinite occupation invites the retort that for hundreds of years Jews were penned into ghettos without resorting to violence. The final, clinching argument is that only anti-Semites expect Jews to behave better than other peoples and who are Christians or Muslims to criticise Israeli actions, after their long record of anti-Jewish persecution?

The Herzl–Freud anecdote is more complicated and more subtle to disentangle. Both protagonists were deracinated cosmopolitans of the type derided by Zionists, viewed critically by practising Jews and suspected by anti-Semites. In Yiddish parlance they were *luftmenshen* (light-as-air men), cast adrift from their Jewish moorings but only grudgingly welcomed in wider society. Yet, to their followers, both were towering geniuses, Freud more genuinely and lastingly so than Herzl. One had a dream, the other interpreted dreams. Herzl sought relief from a troubled inner life in action, Freud revealed the unconscious. Neither was an obvious or admirable icon for the new Zionist movement – indeed, Freud was a critic of it and all nationalisms – but Herzl gave impetus and political credibility to a languishing venture, and Freud, along with Einstein, had to be acknowledged as one of the most original thinkers of the twentieth century, his insights a staple of educational theory in schools and kibbutzim during the Mandate period.

The paradox is that both men transcended, in their lives as well as their careers, the particularist confines of Jewish identity. They were quintessentially Diaspora figures, examples of what the Jew could aspire to and achieve in general society, anti-Semitism notwithstanding. Had they actually lived there, it is doubtful that either would have been able to endure the petty constraints and limited intellectual horizons of state-building in Palestine. Although only marginal Jews if so defined according to their beliefs and practices, they would have missed their European roots and that amalgam of Jewish heritage within wider culture that has been the most significant feature of Jewish Diaspora history since the Enlightenment. Freud spent almost all of his life in a love–hate relationship with Vienna until forced to flee by Nazism and Herzl desperately wanted to 'make it' in the theatre there even more than he wanted to found a state. For them, Vienna was home.

The Zionists, by contrast, were busy erasing the memories of their former homes. On coming to Palestine, they embraced new identities and took on new names, as a sign of rejecting their Diaspora past. Ironically, 'rootless' was their common description for the life of Jews in the Diaspora, but it was the 'new' Jew who had alienated himself from his roots. In a well-known homily recited at the Passover meal that recounts the Exodus story, the ancient rabbis say that, on the strength of four virtues, the Israelites were redeemed from Egypt: they did not change their names, they did not change their language, they did not speak evil, and they did not give up their moral standards. By changing their names and languages into Hebrew (Yiddish was referred to, with jocular contempt, as 'the language of our degradation'), the Zionist pioneers were consciously constructing their new model of the Jew. In so doing, they were blocking out great swathes of Jewish collective memory. Memory is an integral component of Jewish tradition. The Bible contains the verb 'to remember' 169 times in its various declensions, along with numerous injunctions not 'to forget'.[1]

It is a small but telling pointer of cultural difference that nowadays a widespread passion of Diaspora Jews is genealogy; for Israelis it is archaeology. Diaspora genealogy is an attempt to forge links with previous generations and, for many enthusiasts, to fill that great void left by the loss of one in three European Jews during the Holocaust. Israeli archaeology harks back to a distant past, vaulting the intermediate centuries, in order to establish and authenticate an ancient connection with the land. The two millennia and more of Diaspora history that separate ancient from modern Israel are lightly skated over, like an unfortunate interlude between past and present ownership of the territory promised to Abraham.

But, as any amateur psychologist knows, burying or being ashamed of one's past leads to a crisis of identity. It is akin to the embarrassment of first-generation children whose parents speak the acquired language with a foreign accent. As with individuals, so it is with groups. An unresolved past causes an internal splitting, with the bad being projected outwards towards whichever amorphous enemy, whether the Arabs who all want to drive us into the sea or the anti-Semites disguised as anti-Zionists who all want to do away with the Jewish state. The vehement refusal of most Israelis and Diaspora Zionists to concede the validity of the Palestinian narrative – that the Israeli triumph in 1948 was the Palestinian tragedy – suggests that the 'miraculous' solution that Chaim Weizmann had detected in the flight of 600–700,000 Palestinian refugees hides a darker reality that is still too raw to acknowledge. It was Freud who insisted that we are our past; unless it is incorporated and dealt with, there will be an inevitable 'return of the repressed', in his phrase.

The dilemma for an artificially constructed identity is that, in order to assert itself, it must be rigid and inflexible. It cannot allow in too much of the past. There can be no room for ambivalence. The collective Israeli character is direct, forceful, straightforward and untrammelled by doubt, a masculine archetype that, it must be said, most Israeli women adhere to as well. It sees things in black and white. Were peace ever to come between Israelis and Palestinians, it is difficult to imagine Israel consenting to the equivalent of South Africa's Truth and Reconciliation Commission. To do so would require admission of complex moral issues and ambiguous actions in the past and call into question that laboriously compiled construct of the 'new' Jew since pre-state days – the strong but compassionate warrior, armoured in the utter rectitude of his cause, who weeps even as he fires his rifle.

In contrast, ambivalence lies at the heart of Diaspora identity. A recent book by Yuri Slezkine, provocatively entitled *The Jewish Century*, explores the close links between Russian Jews and the Russian Revolution (en passant, it also provides many novel interpretations of the history of Jews in the United States and Palestine–Israel). It is noteworthy that Soviet and Jewish histories of the twentieth century have tended to deal perfunctorily with the Jewish contribution to Russia, except in the context of its anti-Semitic element, especially under Stalin, thus reinforcing two conventional views, one apologetic, the other accusatory: either that Communism was the first system to introduce ethnic and national equality within the Soviet Union, or that Russia, under whatever form of government, has never known how to deal with its large Jewish minority.

Slezkine invents a category, 'Mercurians', to describe Jews and other wandering peoples who provide skills and services to the natives they live among. Mercury, the Roman god of oratory, skill, trading (and thieving), is identified with Hermes, 'the god of all those who did not herd animals, till the soil or live by the sword; the patron of rule-breakers, border-crossers and go-betweens; the protector of people who lived by their wit, craft and art'. There could be no better description of the historical function of Diaspora Jewry. Mercurians, the description continues, 'were transients and wanderers – from fully nomadic Gypsy groups to mostly commercial communities divided into fixed brokers and travelling agents, to permanently settled populations who thought of themselves as exiles. Whether they knew no homeland... or had lost it, like the Armenians and the Jews, or had no political ties to it... they were perpetual resident aliens and vocational foreigners.'

Russian–Jewish history is almost invariably categorised as a long tale of victimisation under the tsars, culminating in the quota system introduced in the 1880s that effectively blocked opportunities for Jewish advancement. Repressive legislation was in force, residence was mainly limited to the Pale of Settlement and there were frequent, terrifying pogroms, often initiated or tacitly condoned by ineffective central authorities seeking to deflect popular unrest onto traditional scapegoats.

Even so, Slezkine points out that the ardent Zionist Vladimir Jabotinsky, educated in the liberal environment of Odessa, lamented in 1903 that 'many, too many of us, children of the Jewish intelligentsia, are madly, shamefully in love with Russian culture'. His grace and fluency in writing the language caused Maxim Gorky to observe that Zionism's gain was Russian literature's loss.

Jews played a prominent part in the 1917 Revolution and were the largest single ethnic group in the Party leadership of the 1920s. The Jews of the Ukraine suffered appallingly in the civil war that followed the October Revolution. When fighting finally ceased at the beginning of 1921, at least 60,000 Jews had been killed by rampaging Ukrainian battalions, the White Army and marauding peasant guerrillas. But, by taking advantage of emancipation, Jews became the best-educated national group in the Soviet Union by 1939. Less than two per cent of the total population, they constituted more than fourteen per cent of all Soviet citizens with higher education. Thirty-three per cent of young Jewish men and women aged between 19 and 24 were college students, compared to five per cent of that age group in the general population. In Moscow and Leningrad, they comprised roughly seventy per cent of dentists, forty per cent of doctors, thirty per cent of writers, journalists and the publishing profession and almost twenty per cent of scientists and university professors – a pre-eminence as marked as that of German Jews before the rise of Nazism. It should also be noted that there was a particularly high proportion of Jewish officers in the security services, almost forty per cent of the NKVD's (the Soviet secret police) top officials in 1937. Who sharper than a Jew, instincts honed by centuries of survival, to detect equivocation in others?

The great purges of the late 1930s and Stalin's post-war, anti-Semitic paranoia once again evoked parallels with tsarist treatment of the Jews, especially in the United States, for obvious reasons of ideological antipathy. But these new attempts to limit Jewish upward mobility and inclusion within the intellectual elite met with only mixed success. Jews remained the most achieving of all Soviet nationalities, with the proportion of college graduates five times higher than among Russians. As the dissident movement emerged in the 1970s, Jews played as prominent a part in it as they had in pre-1917 revolutionary circles. Their right to emigrate, a privilege unavailable to almost every other Soviet citizen, was taken up in the West as a battle of the Cold War. It could be argued that the international publicity given to the cause of refuseniks was one of the factors that led to the Soviet regime's loss of authority and eventual collapse in 1991.

On my two trips to visit refuseniks in the 1980s, in a wary and deeply distrustful atmosphere, with Russians reluctant to meet a foreigner's gaze or engage with them for fear of incrimination, I was sure that I could always pick out the Jewish faces on the buses, in the subway and on the street. In that physiognomically diverse landscape, with Mongol, Tatar and Slav features adding to the astonishing variety, there was something about the intelligence, the vivacity, the alertness of Jewish faces that marked their owners out from the stolid and subdued majority, who, herd-like, went about their business with averted eyes. Russian women knew it too. Despite the discrimination against them, Jewish men were sought-after husbands. They had a reputation for not drowning their sorrows in drink or beating their wives. Perhaps the transmitted abilities that have enabled Diaspora Jews to survive, prevail and flourish are more admirably seen in adversity than in prosperity. It was the ancient rabbis who compared Jews to the olive; the more it is pounded, the finer the oil that it produces.

This mercurial quality of adapting to the environment and making the most of it is evident nowadays in modern Russia. Jews are prominent among the so-called 'oligarchs' who have made their fortunes since the collapse of centralised state control. They are playing a risky game, reminiscent of the situation in the 1920s, when the short-lived Soviet business class was predominantly Jewish, but Jews have characteristically always been the leaven in the Russian bread, an essential but resented ingredient. Maxim Gorky bitingly dismissed the lower ranks of the Communist Party as being filled with 'old Russian nationalists, scoundrels and vagabonds who despise and fear the Jews'. For Bolsheviks, as for Marx himself, Jews as a social group were synonymous with capitalism. At the same time, in America they were looked upon as dangerously prone to Socialism and radical trade unionism.

That is the problem for quick-witted, mobile Mercurians; their intellectual capacity and mercantile talents will always mark them out for suspicion, envy and hostility, whether under totalitarianism or democracy. To the anti-Semite and other segments of the lumpenproletariat, Jews are simultaneously the lowest of the low and taking over all the organs of power as part of a worldwide conspiracy. This was a compelling reason, said the Russian–Jewish pioneers who argued that Zionism was the only solution, for Jews to emigrate en masse to their national homeland. Force of circumstances has seen to it that since the early 1990s there has been a huge exodus, mainly to Israel, of almost half of the Soviet Union's four million Jews. Modern Zionist emissaries to the Diaspora warn that there is no cast-iron guarantee from history that conditions can't change elsewhere in Europe or even in the United States.

Certainly, the State of Israel provides the focal point for a concrete, physically rooted expression of Jewish continuity. Despite Israel's sense of strategic vulnerability and external threats to her security, she has a reassuring fixedness and apparent permanence, in contrast to the scattered, dependent nature of Diaspora life. The first sovereign Jewish state for over two millennia, exercising the novel circumstance of self-rule, protects its citizens with their own army and governs them with laws passed by a democratically elected Jewish parliament. In Israel, Jews are a natural, unself-conscious majority everywhere, whereas it appears worthy of comment when they congregate in particular neighbourhoods of the major cities in America and Europe. Logic would suggest that the future of the Jewish people and their civilisation of Judaism must lie in Israel.

But there is a strong counter-argument. It can be expressed figuratively in a line among the fragments of the Greek poet Archilochus: 'The fox knows many things, but the hedgehog knows one big thing.' Isaiah Berlin, one of the major Diaspora thinkers of the twentieth century, used it as the title of an essay about Tolstoy and his philosophy of history.[2] Berlin's theory is that there is a fundamental distinction between those people who are fascinated by the infinite variety of things (foxes) and those who relate everything to a central, all-embracing system (hedgehogs). In Jewish terms, it is the distinction between those who choose to take their chances in the Diaspora and those who require the security of living in a Jewish state.

The nationalist pursuit of statehood, especially the Zionist version that underpins Israel, is monist, an ideological hedgehog. The concept of Diaspora existence, especially in its Jewish version, is multifaceted, an ideological fox. By nature Zionism is an absolutist project – all or nothing, everything subsumed under statism – whereas by nature the Diaspora response is relativist, depending on the given situation. Diaspora Jews are the fluid, sure-footed followers of Mercury. Israeli Jews are the settled, state-building, law-making followers of Apollo, Mercury's counterpart. The Jew who is stimulated by pluralism and would cite Moses Maimonides, Einstein, Freud and Kafka as just four out of thousands of similar examples of Jews enhanced by their contact with wider culture, will opt for life in the United States or Europe. An Israeli who feels constrained by cultural particularism of the Zionist or religiously Orthodox brand will envy and seek to emulate. From earliest times, talented and ambitious people have always been drawn to the challenges and opportunities of the big city. Small countries invariably lose their brightest citizens to emigration.

The Jewish fox knows many things; the Jewish hedgehog knows only one big thing. One has gained his wisdom over centuries of responding to dispersion, persecution and adaptation; the other is still learning to fend for himself, with no previous experience to draw upon. When Hamlet cautioned Horatio that there were more things in heaven and earth than dreamt of in his philosophy, he could have been a Diaspora Jew vainly trying to give the benefit of experience to an Israeli.

The Zionist is right in warning that Jewish history gives no cast-iron guarantees. 'I was no prophet, neither was I a prophet's son,' the biblical Amos indignantly tells his accusers. Nevertheless, if asked to choose where the future survival of Jewry is more likely to be safeguarded – in the dispersion, variety and exigencies of Jewish life in the Diaspora or in a nationalist Jewish state claiming to act and speak for all of the world's Jews in their manifold diversity – the Jewish majority still opts for the former and certainly prefers to live there. Zionism is as defensible and justifiable as any other national movement; given the insecurities of European Jewish existence when it emerged, probably more so, but nationalism per se is neither particularly praiseworthy nor condemnable – it is morally neutral. As Nachman Syrkin, an early Zionist theoretician, defined it, it is a particular 'category' of history, not an absolute. For better or for worse, centuries of living in the Diaspora have turned Jews into universalists rather than particularists, and it is in championing universal values that we continue to make our most distinctive contribution in the struggle for human progress.

NOTES

Chapter 1

1 Salo Baron, 'Ghetto and Emancipation', *Menorah Journal* 14 (June 1928)
2 Emil Fackenheim, 'Jewish Values in the Post-Holocaust Future', *Judaism* 16 (Summer 1967)

Chapter 2

1 *Shevet Yehudah* (The Rod of Judah), first printed in Adrianople in 1550, with additions written by Solomon's son, Joseph

Chapter 5

1 For a fuller treatment of rabbinic responses to the Bar Kochba revolt and Messianism generally, see chapter 2, *Power and Powerlessness in Jewish History* by David Biale (Schocken Books, London, 1986)

Chapter 6

1 Translated in Yitzhak F. Baer, *History of the Jews in Christian Spain*, 2 vols (Jewish Publication Society, Philadelphia), vol. 2, p.77

2 Quoted in Eliyahu Ashtor, *The Jews of Moslem Spain*, 2 vols (Jewish Publication Society, Philadelphia), vol. 1, p.176
3 See *The Penguin Book of Hebrew Verse*, edited and translated by T. Carmi (Allen Lane and Penguin Books, London, 1981)
4 R. Moses Hacohen, *Ezer ha-Emunah* (1375), quoted in Yitzhak F. Baer, *History of the Jews in Christian Spain*, vol. 1, p.374

Chapter 7

1 Giovanni da Anagni, *In librum quintum decretalium* (Milan, 1492), quoted in David Biale, *Power and Powerlessness in Jewish History*, p.63

Chapter 9

1 Theodor Herzl, *The Jewish State*, translated by Harry Zohn (Herzl Press, New York, 1970)
2 Isaac Marcus Jost, *Allgemeine Geschichte des Israelitischen Volkes*, vol. 1 (Berlin, 1832), sections translated in Michael Meyer, *Ideas of Jewish History* (Behrman House, New York, 1974)

Chapter 10

1 Leo Pinsker, *Auto-Emancipation*, substantially reproduced in Arthur Hertzberg, *The Zionist Idea* (Atheneum, New York, 1959)
2 See Oz Almog, *The Sabra: The Creation of the New Jew*, pp.78–80 (University of California Press, Berkeley, 2000)
3 Micah Berdichevsky, *Wrecking and Building* (1900), in Arthur Hertzberg, *The Zionist Idea*, (Jewish Publication Society, Philadelphia, 1997)

Chapter 11

1 'With Yehuda Ya'ari', *Ha-Poel Ha-Tza'ir* 29 (January 1963)
2 Quoted in Jacqueline Rose, 'Freud and the Rise of Zionism', *London Review of Books* (8 July 2004) 26:3
3 Ibid.

Chapter 12

1 Aharon Urinovsky, 'For the Rectification of the Study of the Bible', *Shorashim* 2 (1938): 1
2 Arthur Koestler, *Promise and Fulfilment: Palestine 1905–1931* (Macmillan, London, 1949), p.283
3 Chaim Arieh Zuta and Y. Spibak, *The History of Our People* (Tel Aviv, 1936), 4th edn

Chapter 13

1 Max Weber, *Politics as a Vocation*, in H. H. Gerth and C. Wright Mills, eds, *From Max Weber* (OUP, New York, 1946)
2 Ruppin to Hans Kohn, quoted in Susan Lee Hattis, *The Bi-National Idea* (Shikmona, Haifa, 1970), p.48
3 Arthur Ruppin, *My Life and Work* (Tel Aviv, 1968), p.149

Chapter 14

1 David Ben-Gurion, *Memoirs*, vol. 1, pp.254–255

Chapter 15

1 Letter to Meyer Weisgal, quoted in Aaron Berman, *Nazism, the Jews and American Zionism, 1933–1948* (Wayne State University Press, Detroit, 1990), pp.107–108
2 Shabtai Teveth, *Ben-Gurion: The Burning Ground, 1886–1948* (Houghton Mifflin, Boston, 1987), p.854
3 Moshe Tabenkin, quoted in Yoav Gelber, 'Zionist Policy and the Fate of European Jewry, 1943–44', *Studies in Zionism* 7 (Spring 1983)
4 Samuel Lubell, 'The Second Exodus of the Jews', *Saturday Evening Post* (5 October 1946)
5 Quoted by M. Lissak, 'The Image of Immigrants: Stereotypes and Labels during the Mass Immigration of the Fifties', *Katedra* 43 (1987)
6 See, for examples, Oz Almog, *The Sabra: The Creation of the New Jew*, pp.88–90

7 Shabtai Teveth, *Ben-Gurion: The Burning Ground, 1886–1948*, p.853
8 Eric Alterman, 'West Bank Story', *Present Tense* 16 (March–April 1989)
9 Dan Raviv and Yossi Melman, *Friends in Deed: Inside the US–Israel Alliance* (Hyperion, New York, 1994)
10 Yehuda Bauer, *The Jewish Emergence from Powerlessness* (University of Toronto Press, Toronto, 1979), p.68
11 David J. Goldberg, *To the Promised Land: A History of Zionist Thought* (Penguin Books, London, 1996), p.250
12 David Vital, 'After the Catastrophe: Aspects of Contemporary Jewry', in *Lessons and Legacies: The Meaning of the Holocaust in a Changing World*, ed. Peter Hayes (Northwestern University Press, Evanston, Ill., 1991)

Chapter 16

1 Peter Novick, *The Holocaust and Collective Memory* (Bloomsbury, London, 1999), p.147
2 See, for example, Jeremy Bowen, *Six Days: How the 1967 War Shaped the Middle East* (Simon & Schuster, London, 2003), pp.52–53, or Shlomo Gazit, *Trapped Fools* (Frank Cass, London, 2003), p.xiii

Chapter 17

1 Quoted in Jeremy Bowen, *Six Days: How the 1967 War Shaped the Middle East*, pp.323–324

Chapter 18

1 Quoted in Peter Novick, *The Holocaust and Collective Memory*, p.149

Chapter 19

1 Meier Shalev, quoted in Allison Kaplan Sommer, 'Two-Four-Six-Eight, We Deserve a Jewish State', *Jerusalem Post* (15 July 1994)
2 Ze'ev Schiff, *A History of the Israeli Army, 1874 to the Present* (Macmillan, New York, 1985)
3 When, in 1978, I had written an article in *The Times* for the festival of Passover suggesting that the Palestinians, too, deserved their freedom, the outraged denunciations from Anglo-Jewry's communal organisations made me feel relieved that I was absent in Italy for three months on a mini-sabbatical.

Chapter 21

1 Quoted in Baruch Kimmerling, *Politicide: Ariel Sharon's War against the Palestinians* (Verso, London, 2003), p.17
2 Ibid. p.39
3 'The Truth from the Land of Israel', *Complete Works of Achad Ha-Am* (Tel Aviv, 1946), p.23

Chapter 22

1 Peter Novick, *The Holocaust and Collective Memory*, p.10
2 Isaiah Berlin, *The Hedgehog and the Fox: An Essay on Tolstoy's View of History* (Weidenfeld & Nicolson, London, 1953)

BIBLIOGRAPHY AND ACKNOWLEDGEMENTS

Both of the books, and their extensive bibliographies, written previously about Jewish history (*The Jewish People: Their History and Their Religion* [co-authored with John D. Rayner], Viking 1987, Penguin Books 1989) and Zionist ideology (*To the Promised Land: A History of Zionist Thought*, Penguin Books, 1996) furnished me with the historical material that I have made use of in this work. I do not claim that it is a piece of original scholarship, rather an exploration in the realm of ideas, which is why I have deliberately kept footnote references to a minimum. As a non-specialist in most fields, I find that constantly having to refer to notes is irksome and I imagine that the general reader, for whom this book is primarily intended, feels likewise.

The theme of the widening divide between Israel and the Diaspora germinated over several years, during which time, mainly as the senior rabbi of a distinguished liberal congregation, I became increasingly exercised over the dilemma of supporting a Jewish state whose political behaviour was often at odds with Judaism's ethical teachings. A growing number of Jews, religious and humanist, within Israel or outside, expressed similar reservations. To publicise these concerns was deemed 'giving comfort to Israel's enemies' or 'washing dirty linen in public' but vigorous debate is the lifeblood of democracy and Jews are disputatious by temperament, so I feel no contrition about my regular forays into the media. If in some small way they cause people to think again about the standard fare put out in Israel and the Diaspora by government information departments, pressure groups, public relations agencies and venal journalists, it will be worth the hostility they sometimes occasion, when at issue is the ethos of the first Jewish state in two thousand years and the nature of the Israel–Diaspora relationship.

It was reassuring in the course of reading to come across authors who dealt with themes that converged with my own ideas and I wish to acknowledge five books in particular for their contribution to this text.

The first is *Power and Powerlessness in Jewish History* by David Biale (Schocken Books, 1986). It is a radical re-interpretation of the myth of Jewish political passivity between the fall of an independent commonwealth in 70 CE and the rebirth of the State of Israel in 1948. Biale was a valuable source of information about the structures of Jewish communal organisation and defence in the Middle Ages and beyond.

Peter Novick's *The Holocaust and Collective Memory* (Bloomsbury, 1999) is a provocative and iconoclastic study of responses to the Holocaust and how they have been manipulated since the end of the Second World War to shape any debate about Israel and the Diaspora.

The Sabra: The Creation of the New Jew by Oz Almog (University of California Press, 2000) is a comprehensive sociological analysis of the making by the early Zionists of a new Jewish 'type' that defines the modern Israeli personality and their reaction to Diaspora history.

Amos Elon's *The Pity of It All: A Portrait of German Jews 1743–1933* (Allen Lane, 2003) is an important work of historical restoration, chronicling a period of cultural achievement and social integration that produced a Diaspora golden age greater than that of Spanish Jewry in its heyday.

Finally, *Israel: A History* by Martin Gilbert (Doubleday, 1998) is a sympathetic, magisterial account of the origins and development of the Jewish state from early pioneering days to the fiftieth anniversary of its establishment. It was an invaluable resource for facts and details about events since the 1982 Lebanon War.

These five books provided my basic sources and I gratefully record my debt to them, although any perspective on the material they contain is my own, as is the interpretation I bring to Jewish history generally and the nature of the Israel–Diaspora relationship today.

It was Turi Munthe who first approached me about writing such a book, overcame my initial reservations about dipping my toes, yet again, into controversial waters, patiently awaited my recovery from a serious illness to begin writing and gently coaxed me towards completion of the final manuscript. I do hope that his confidence in the project was not misplaced. Willie and Jo Kessler, two generous friends, allowed me to use their apartment on the beautiful Dorset coast in Thomas Hardy country as an ideal location in which to think, walk and write.

As always, my wife Carole-Ann provided encouragement, companionship and a corrective flick of the whip whenever I was tempted by too many transient distractions. Her loving support and principled integrity has sustained me, our children and my career over thirty-six years. In her I have been blessed indeed.

David J. Goldberg
London, April 2005

INDEX